## Dedication

This book is dedicated to those who devote their lives to education, especially those who shared their experienced insights in the publication of this book.

**Sowhat Imprint**
Email: **sowhatimprint@gmail.com**

Website **www.sowhat.ie**

© Mark Hamilton 2021

All rights reserved. No part of this publication may be reproduced or transmitted in any form or by any means, electronic or mechanical, including photocopying, recording or any information storage or retrieval system, without prior permission from the publishers.

First published 2021.

*British Library Cataloguing-in-Publication Data*
A catalogue record for this book is available from the British Library.
ISBN 978-1-8382579-3-4

Typeset, printed and bound by:
W&G Baird Ltd, Greystone Press, Antrim BT41 2DU

# OUR SCHOOL IS CATHOLIC SO WHAT?

MARK HAMILTON

● ● SO WHAT
● ● IMPRINT

# Contents

| | |
|---|---|
| Introduction | 7 |
| | |
| **Section 1 – Setting the scene** | **15** |
| 1. Aspects of the Irish educational landscape | 16 |
| 2. Light and shade – as seen through Catholic eyes | 28 |
| | |
| **Section 2 – The difference a God makes** | **35** |
| 3. Understanding the Catholic-Christian worldview | 36 |
| 4. Secularist worldviews | 41 |
| 5. Contrasting and competing | 46 |
| 6. The impact of the secular outlook on education | 53 |
| | |
| **Section 3 – The added value of Catholicism** | **61** |
| 7. What Catholic-Christianity contributes to modern society | 62 |
| 8. How a Catholic education prepares a student for life | 72 |
| 9. What constitutes a Catholic ethos in schooling? | 77 |
| | |
| **Section 4 – Catholic education: making it happen** | **85** |
| 10. Helping your school to be Catholic | 86 |
| 11. Are Catholic schools doing anything wrong? | 95 |
| 12. Addressing academic standards | 109 |
| 13. The building blocks of character | 115 |
| 14. Curriculum: what's on the menu? | 124 |
| 15. Educating in prayer life | 133 |
| 16. The school as a professional arena | 140 |

**Section 5 – Current challenges to school ethos**     147
17. The new Framework for Primary Schools     148
18. Relationships and Sexuality Education     151
19. Wellbeing     161
20. ERB and Ethics programmes     165
21. When education becomes political     170

**Section 6 – Appreciating how Catholic education is different**     185
22. Similar language, different identities     186
23. Facing up to the political landscape     198

**Appendix 1**     Implementing character education in schools     207
**Appendix 2**     Developing and maintaining a Catholic standard     221

**Index**     227

# Introduction

> **Key Takeaways**
>
> *For Catholics the aim of education is to help in understanding the purpose and meaning of life. Thus education needs be holistic – seeking to educate all aspects of the person. Included in that are the more functional needs of the future workplace.*
>
> *God's existence changes everything. Reflection on creation and on the life of Christ impact enormously on education.*
>
> *Different worldviews produce different educational models. Catholic education is needed not only by Catholics but also plays a role in buttressing a truly democratic society.*

Many of the key ideas which define Western civilisation derive from Christianity. Unlocking their potential requires an education in Christian values. Consequently, iit is not surprising that Catholic education continues to have worldwide prestige and is highly desirable, even among non-Christians. Yet looking at Irish society today, much of which has been actually shaped by Catholic education, there are strong trends seeking to reject this educational approach.

This book argues that if Ireland, and the Western world, wish to have a democratic future, then Catholic education is needed to underpin it. A waning of the influence of Catholic education will result in a weakening of people's capacity to resist the damaging forces that are eking away at the foundations of democracy.

It is also a major contention of this book that a partial reason for our current societal decline is that Ireland has not got Catholic education quite right, and as a society we require a fuller understanding of what Catholic education actually is.

This book sets out to explain what Catholic education is and how it can be realised. It argues that it is imperative that Catholic education recover its strength

– not just for the wellbeing of those who choose to avail of it, but to strengthen democratic society's resistance to increasingly destructive secularising forces.

## The whole person

A widespread complaint in our modern Western culture is that we are all citizens of an economy and not of a society. Education is viewed pragmatically. It is fundamentally about acquiring the skills necessary to get a job, to earn money, to become consumers. Money is necessary for living, and education is the path to money.

There are additional philosophical ideas at play which lead to this pragmatic approach to education. For some there is no life other than this one – there is no life after death to look forward to. Society then is a fundamentally materialist environment where education is a purely functional guide to help us negotiate our way. The ideal education system supporting this worldview is one which has *functionality* at its heart – one that prepares us all for the workplace, marketplace and for active citizenship, and any other higher things that might be recognised by our secularised culture.

For a different reason many Catholics also buy into a similar functionality when considering schooling. Academic learning is for the here and now, they believe, whereas religion is about life after death. School is where you learn and acquire practical skills, with a view to preparing yourself for the next stage of this life. Religion is an added extra which is addressed only within Religion class. In such an understanding of the world, all education systems are basically the same, that is, functional, except that some schools will provide religion classes and some won't.

Catholic education, as educators well know, has a much broader vision of the task in hand. Human beings are not reducible to random aggregates of atoms but are part of a meaningful creation, with an eternal destiny to be with God. The great aim of education is to equip us to realise that purpose and meaning, the why of our existence. When expressed in this way the direct contrast with the more functional objective of education becomes clear. Catholic education builds up from a foundation of meaning and purpose, whereas for many other educational models such an underpinning is either meaningless – or to be ignored.

# Introduction

Building from such a base, Catholic education is necessarily holistic and integral. It sees the schooling system as a process to educate all aspects of the person, realising that it is the whole person who acts in this world, and who has an eye on future eternal destiny.

## Getting it right

There never was a 'once upon a time' in education when things were exactly as they should be. Nor is there ever full agreement on what schools should seek to achieve. Those deeply involved in educational delivery have a broad appreciation that education is a preparation for life while those at the output end – mainly those awaiting new employees to enter the labour market – see it more as preparing people for the workplace.

The Catholic educational vision over many centuries has adapted to the needs of society, whether in providing the basic literacy needs of the impoverished, educating future society leaders or supplying the ecclesial needs of the Catholic community. It has constantly refined its vision, aware that the 'new Jerusalem' is linked in some fashion to our present world, and that while a perfect society is not achievable here below, humans do have desires for earthly peace and justice which society has a duty to seek to realise.

For the Catholic, God's existence changes everything. The knowledge derived from reflection on our creation added to the wisdom that Christ himself has revealed ensures that human persons are well placed to make noble use of the goods of this world while never losing sight of the next.

This book covers a wide range of aspects of Catholic education and not all parts will be of equal interest to the reader. The division of the book into sections makes it more accessible while allowing readers to delve at will into those areas of most interest. Section 1 sets the scene for Catholicism in Ireland and for Catholic education more widely. Section 2 provides a philosophical background to the secular worldview and contrasts it with a Catholic understanding. Section 3 explains what Catholicism contributes to society and to the individual, and how a Catholic school's ethos facilitates that. Sections 4 and 5 are very practical sections showing how a Catholic school should function as well as outlining some of the challenges schools currently face. The two appendices on Character Education and Maintaining a Catholic Standard have a similar, solid practical intent. Section 6 looks at alternative models to Catholic schooling while reminding us of the advantages of Catholic education. That final section also reviews the current political landscape for schools.

Should a reader require a quick overview of contents, each chapter begins with a list of key takeaways, providing a precis of the content that follows it. It should be noted for accuracy – although it has no practical impact on the book's content – that the book uses the term Catholic school in a slightly wider sense than usually defined. A Catholic school is part of the ministry of the Catholic Church and is subject to some degree of ecclesiastical authority. In this book, the term is used to describe any school that claims to have a Catholic identity.

**Making Catholic education happen**

The worldviews deriving from interest or disinterest in God's existence diverge widely and impact hugely on how education is delivered. Initially, having presented what is of necessity a very brief review of Irish society and Catholic life, the early sections of this book go on to explore the differing worldviews presented by both Catholicism and secularism and how these impact on education.

These contrasting outlooks provide a platform from which one can explain what is termed in Section 3 the 'added value of Catholicism', in which Christianity's contributions to supporting modern democratic society and to the education of the person are fully explored. This naturally leads to a review of what should constitute a Catholic ethos in schooling. Section 4 then examines how such an ethos can enliven a school.

In general Irish schools have not got the balance correct when it comes to Catholic education. This failure may have contributed to some present shortcomings in our society. Included among those identified weaknesses in schools is a lack of focus on character education, which, when it is present, can as much serve as a building block for academic excellence as it can for human and moral maturity. Appendix 1 reviews very practical ways in which a school can deliver on character education.

Aside from any internal difficulties facing Catholic schools that are seeking to be faithful to their ethos, there are also challenges presented by prescribed

# Introduction

curricula. Section 5 looks at the impact a wider secularised culture is having on the curricula for primary and secondary schools and highlights the stark incompatibilities that can arise. Any curriculum formed on the basis of secularist assumptions directly destabilises the Catholic integral approach to education. The essential unity of knowledge on which Catholic education is based is undermined by the new draft Framework for Primary Schools as well as by aspects of the new Wellbeing and proposed RSE programmes. A question is asked – why does a political system so keen on a diversity of school type insist on undermining that diversity – and thereby parental choice – through a lack of respect for school autonomy and through a mandated curriculum?

Section 6 turns to the question of language and how the purposes of education and schooling are explained to parents. Evolving definitions are a key element in undermining or disguising true meanings.

Woke politics, which has been simmering for many years, is now bursting out across many aspects of Western society. The term 'woke' derives from the idea of being awake to injustice. Woke politics provides a reductionist view of society as comprising of disparate groups who are in an oppressor-oppressed relationship with each other. Woke thinking proposes to repair society by the silencing of oppressor groups and the destruction of anything that leads to dominance of one group over another.

This emerging woke culture is examined, as are the way it leads to the politicisation of schooling. Some current political questions are looked at, such as the international pressure for secular schooling, the plan for school divestment, and how to deal with diversity and with opt-outs on conscience grounds. More straightforwardness rather than political manipulation is called for.

This book aims to clarify for parents, teachers and students the great value to be acquired from a Catholic education, no matter the background of the individual student. It can serve as a guidebook in helping educationalists work to fulfil the vision of a Catholic education in their school. It can also be of help to other Christian denominations who have a strong appreciation for the ethos of their institutions.

In these turbulent times the Coronavirus has exposed many vulnerabilities within our society, while highlighting that humanity's strongest asset is the care we show to others. A Catholic school's insistence on 'above all, charity' should guide it in being steadfast in its ethos, advancing a truly Catholic culture with a view to ensuring that education properly serves the long-term needs of persons, families, civic society, the Christian community and our wider democratic institutions.

**Realism or optimism**

Fr Brendan Kilcoyne, a west of Ireland parish priest and former school principal, started his own podcast series during the 2020 lockdown as a contribution to the re-Christianisation of Ireland. He has expressed some pessimism about the possibilities for the future of Catholic education. In an interview promoting his podcast he said: 'I worry that the education system has killed our love of learning though. I saw as a teacher what Pearse called the "murder machine".… You're supposed to give people a thirst, a drought, an intellectual thirst, and in a Catholic school that should be both intellectual and spiritual. The two cannot be separated, and we haven't yet cracked it.'

'We've lost our schools, which isn't a judgement on any teachers, but Irish Catholicism as a body has been taken by a fever and is in its final crisis.' added Kilcoyne.

In that same interview Kilcoyne acknowledges Ireland's huge missionary outreach, 'where that impulse to service and nobility was most expended. And at home we were burned out.'

Another way of viewing the current malaise is to acknowledge that despite all the difficulties there is a strong Catholic laity within Ireland who have a deep appreciation for much of what Catholic education can deliver and have a strong impulse to 'service and nobility'. Intellectual and spiritual thirsts can both be comprehensively slaked at schools which strive to achieve the goals outlined in this book, although this requires robust efforts by parents, teachers and managements to make it happen. Like the Irish missionaries of the past these need not be many in number but they must epitomise the spirit of service they wish to inspire. Optimists may be right to doubt Fr Kilcoyne's judgement, but they will revert to adopting his realism should there fail to be a Catholic renaissance in response to the upcoming educational threats identified in this book.

# Introduction

***Endnotes***

**Realism or optimism:** for more information see *Podcasting priest bares soul of Irish Catholicism* by Tim Jackson Mar 14, 2021 – an interview with Fr Brendan Kilcoyne (on www.gript.ie)

# SECTION 1
# Setting the scene

At a time when a secular culture is taking a stronger hold in Ireland, Catholic education is at a crossroads. Schools wishing to live up to their Catholic characteristic spirit experience many outside negative pressures, not least from proposed curriculum change.

Despite being a driver of high educational standards, Catholic education is now deemed unwanted by some secularists. Additionally, some Catholics lack the conviction that Catholic education is worth defending. Yet while there are ongoing demands that more Catholic schools be divested, many parents are showing little desire for changes.

In this first section the international prestige of Catholic education is examined, including its success in Ireland. A brief review of the quality and reputation of the service currently being provided is undertaken as well as previewing some of the changes that are in the offing. Chapter 2 addresses the evident religious decline happening in Ireland while acknowledging the many silver linings. Consideration is also given to the secular hostility directed at Catholicism, especially in the mainstream media.

# Chapter 1
# Aspects of the Irish educational landscape

> *Key Takeaways*
>
> *Ireland's political leaders want a plurality of school types but education authorities do not seem to be willing to allow for diversity within school curricula.*
>
> *An apparently underfunded Irish education system has strong international prestige.*
>
> *Past wrongs of Catholic institutions are repugnant to committed Christians. Catholic institutions are at their best when aligned with Gospel values, not with the prevailing culture.*
>
> *Internationally, Catholic schools perform well – they provide what employers and parents seek, and are in high demand. The throwaway society in which we live provides strong grounds for people to choose Catholic schools, yet our media seems to wish that Catholic schools align themselves more with the wider secular culture.*
>
> *The Constitution regards the family as the primary and natural educator of the child and Catholic educators concur. Catholic education provides a vaccine for the turbulence in our modern world.*

**Change is in the air**

The Irish education system is currently in a period of transition. Changes that are made now are expected to last a generation or longer. Paradoxically, education authorities are currently seeking to achieve plurality among schooling types while undermining diversity within school curricula. In the words of the 2020 Programme of Government the aim is 'to increase parental choice' yet the thrust of the curriculum is to ensure a one-size-fits-all approach. That such a deep paradox can persist at national level is a clear warning that the survival of Catholic schooling will depend on its protagonists communicating its raison d'etre clearly to wider society.

## Aspects of the Irish educational landscape

As the number of Irish persons identifying as being Catholic declines (78% of the population identified as Catholic in the most recent census), and as secularist voices are more readily heard in the mainstream media, there is an increasing clamour for divestment of further Catholic primary schools to the state. The 2020 Programme for Government is committed to expanding the plurality of schools, aiming to achieve a target of at least 400 multi-denominational primary schools by 2030, 'so as to improve parental choice'. On the other hand, there is a small but steadily increasing number of families choosing to home-school their children because they do not appreciate secular influences in their local Catholic schools.

At primary level, the National Council for Curriculum and Assessment (NCCA) is in the process of developing a new framework for primary school education (called the draft Framework for Primary Schools in this book). At second level, the newly developed Junior Cycle programme continues to bed down, and the NCCA are steadily coming to grips with the compulsory Wellbeing programme. The growing tensions between the new Junior Cycle objectives and the existing exam-driven Senior Cycle will come into much sharper focus over the next couple of years as the 2022 Leaving Certificate exam becomes the first ever high-stakes examination many students will have faced.

Senior-cycle reform has been long in the making but significant change has yet to happen. The Covid-19 pandemic has clearly exposed the unsuitable, highly inflexible nature of the Leaving Certificate. Third-level college-entry reform has been promised for years but all that has happened to date has been a tinkering around the edges of the CAO points system. The Organisation for Economic Co-Operation and Development (OECD) has recently condemned the Leaving Certificate as unfit for purpose, describing it as 'too narrow and rigid' and the OECD also stated that it was not clear how the Irish education system 'prepares students for a future beyond the Leaving Certificate'. Emerging changes that are expected at the time of writing include the publication of the NCCA's new Framework for Primary Schools and the NCCA's commitment to produce a new relationships and sexuality programme (RSE) for schools.

**Quality education despite apparent under-investment**

Against this evolving educational background, Irish schools just work away and do what schools do – provide an education for students which, judged by PISA standards, is of a high quality.

The Programme for International Student Assessment (PISA) results for 2018 show Ireland's 15-year-olds are among the best in Europe in reading literacy and are performing significantly higher than the other European (OECD) countries average in mathematics and science. The 2016 Programme for Government stated that

> Ireland is recognised as having a strong education system, with a well-trained and committed teaching profession. Our rates of school completion and participation in higher education continue to rise.

This PISA success appears to be above expectations given that our investment in education is poor – at least when measured as a percentage of our Gross National Product. In 2015, 3.8% of Irish GDP was spent on education compared to 5% for the EU28 average, although if the new 'alternative' to GDP is considered, that is, the Gross National Income or GNI – which seeks to exclude 'unreal' effects of multinationals – then the 2015 Irish figure rises to 6.1% and puts Ireland's investment among the top six in investment in education in Europe. If we were to seek to measure educational investment solely by the teacher-student ratio then at both primary level and secondary level Ireland rates below the EU28 average.

As regards the state's investment in the various types of school the overall picture is not straightforward. Amidst that complexity there are some clear trends. Most state primary schools, the vast majority of which are under religious patronage, rely on additional fundraising by parents to make ends meet. And Catholic voluntary secondary schools are among the most poorly state-funded school type, constituting what would appear to be a tolerated but clear, long-standing discrimination.

**World-wide reputation of Catholic schools**

It is an acceptable generalisation to say that, worldwide, Catholic schools are much sought-after institutions. In many developing countries the Catholic Church has been, and is, the biggest non-state provider of education by far, often doing so on help supplied by under-resourced, local Catholic parishes.

In advanced countries Catholic education has strong prestige. For example, Hong Kong is among the top-rated countries in the world for educational attainment as determined by PISA scores. Although only 5% of its population is Catholic, over 20% of school-age children attend Catholic schools there.

Insofar as one seeks to evaluate Irish Catholic schools based on Leaving Certificate attainment (perhaps an unwise measure as it is redolent of infamous school league tables), Catholic schools perform very well. The same is true of Catholic schools in Northern Ireland and in the British system of education. Despite a clamour here for divestment of Catholic primary schools to the state, the glacial progress being made suggests that the high reputation of Catholic education is a delaying factor. It is one thing to consider a change of school patron, but will it be for the better?

Why does being Catholic enhance a school's reputation in so many instances? Results do play a part – academic results often being associated with approaches to learning. It may also be that Catholic schools ordinarily give parents – apart from academic results – what they want. Most parents want schools to reflect the values of the home or to at least acknowledge the importance of these. They like schools that support and value families; that commit to community; schools that instil faith, even if the families themselves don't fully share that faith. In general, students from Catholic schools show high levels of civic engagement, they are supportive of civil liberties, they have high educational expectations, resulting in fewer behavioural problems. Whatever that Catholic mix is, it generally works.

In turn, when one looks at what employers seek, they generally want well-rounded young people, who can work as part of a team, who are critical thinkers, who can share in decision making and problem solving, and who have good communication skills. These are also characteristics that parents want, as they help in a young person's success. Catholic schools can provide young people with these skills by the bucketful.

**What are the features of a Catholic school?**

While educational standards and educational investment are important considerations for everyone involved in education these are not the direct focus of this publication. Nor is it seeking to claim that Catholic schools – by virtue of being Catholic – automatically guarantee better educational results than other schools. The purpose is to dwell on what exactly makes a school Catholic, on why that matters – a lot – in today's society, on ideas on how a school 'ethos' or 'characteristic spirit' can be performative, and why it behoves Catholic schools to seek to be coherently Catholic. Being Catholic makes a difference – and perhaps the insights from this book will help one understand why.

What is a Catholic ethos school? What does it mean for a school to claim to have it? How does a school realise it? What are the challenges schools face in maintaining it? Is it important in our secular world? Does it make any difference to the good of society as a whole?

As one works one's way through these chapters, it will become obvious that many of the ideas therein will be seen to apply wholly or in part to schools of other Christian denominations, allowing this book and its argument to have a wider appeal.

**Is there a demand for Catholic schools?**

The demand for Catholic schools seems robust as judged by enrolment, by the general lack of enthusiasm for the school divestment process, and by the degree of engagement of Catholic primary schools with diocesan authorities on reinforcing their schools' characteristic spirits.

That said, not everyone in Ireland wants Catholic schools for their children. The demand for education in a non-religious environment is steadily growing, with a significant 9.8% of the population describing themselves in the 2016 Census as having no religion. The 2020 Programme for Government acknowledges the continual under-supply of such schools, and will address it, as was said, by providing at least 400 multidenominational primary schools by 2030.

Additionally there is a decreasing esteem for religion in society as well as decreasing religious practice. A tarnished Catholic image together with arguable selective reporting of the past have made many people ashamed of their history, spurring on a reason to change.

There is also a growing home-school movement in Ireland, which had been increasing by around 5% annually, and which has now received a very strong Covid-19 boost. Three times as many families sought to home school in 2020/21 as in the previous year. Excluding that surge, the steady growth alone suggests that for a variety of reasons people are not satisfied with the education being imparted in any of the school types available.

**Addressing the past**

It is not the focus of this book to address the past wrongs of Catholicism, or the substantial failures of individuals, structures and organisations in this country, other than to say that all organisations, be they state-run or religious, can display pathologies. Where Catholic institutions may profess higher standards it is good that they are held to these.

Societies do need to be continually learning from their complex pasts. Yet when the historical record is shaped by a narrative which is primarily seeking to undermine religious loyalties then very little can be learned. An even-handed Mother and Baby Homes Report produced in early 2021 was twisted by many elements among the Irish media to unjustly decry the Catholic Church and all religious influence, providing a media narrative of how that past should be seen rather than how it was. Not happy that the Commission laid the blame at the door of the wider Irish society, the media sought to stoke anti-Catholic prejudice.

Most media reviews of 20th century institutional abuse (and personal abuse) in Ireland have been dominated by this anti-religious and anti-Catholic narrative, so it can be hard to assess what actually went wrong. Harrowing genuine personal stories testify to cruel, hard, unjust and inhumane treatment in religious (mainly Catholic) and state institutions, which are repugnant and not understandable to many coherent Christians.

International comparisons are seldom made, and if this were to happen, the issues might be better contextualised. By way of comparison, a 2020 Report on abuse in New Zealand institutions (faith-based and state care) from the 1960s to early 2000s found that 250,000 young people or vulnerable adults were abused, which accounts for 40% of the total in care during that time, with most abuse happening in the 1970s and 1980s. 'The likelihood of children and young people abused in faith-based or religious homes ranges from 21% to 42%'. This specific statistic in this case might then seem to indicate that there were relatively more incidents of abuse in state institutions as compared with faith-based institutions.

That said, Catholics should expect that Catholic institutions and individuals would seek to set higher standards for society. When Catholic institutions do not live up live up to Gospel values this needs to be called out, and deference to authority is never a sufficient defence. Many historical failures arose when Catholic institutions aligned themselves too closely with the prevailing culture, often reflecting the prejudices of the wider society. For example, in the middle of the last century, Frank Duff's Legion of Mary would appear to have adopted a more Gospel-based approach to the people they were serving than many religious institutions who were seeking to address the same problem.

A similar challenge of rising above the culture is now facing Catholic educational institutions. It is imperative that schools today which claim to be Catholic seek to uphold and impart the high standards set by Jesus Christ and not water these down by succumbing to the obviously inadequate cultural mores of our present age. Looking back on today's Catholic schooling in a century's time one would wish to see it as an education system which had been enriched and imbued by Catholic principles, and not one which, through a failure of nerve, had conspired with secular influences in the decline of democratic society and of the Catholic faith.

## The ingredients for success

As will become clear throughout this book, despite the relative success of Catholic education there are growing pressures on Catholic schools to change, so to speak, or to align better with the wider culture. With so much change in the air, this book challenges people to reflect on what actually is different about Catholic education, and why it is worth continuing to foster that difference. How can parents, teachers and students help their school to live up to its Catholic ethos? Are there practical day-to-day steps that will enhance school ethos leading to better outcomes for all students? Section Four in this book could be viewed as providing the beginnings of a checklist for success.

The undoubted accomplishments of our educational system, which is often touted as an attractive feature for foreign direct investment (FDI) in Ireland, has not lessened the push to make Catholic schools less Catholic. Why so? If any corporation could boast a success rate in its subsidiaries similar to that in Irish schools – as judged by PISA – it would be slow to interfere with their workings. Not so when it comes to education in Ireland, and Catholic education in particular. What are the current external threats that might undermine this Catholic ethos, and how might these be successfully managed?

This book will argue that the holistic approach of Catholic education is a vital ingredient in its educational success. Given the current application of market principles to third-level education, and the increasing fragmentation of knowledge occurring there, the value of the learning acquired at first and second level has grown in importance. As the culture of our society grows steadily out of step with a Catholic insight into reality, the role of the Catholic school for the individual, for family, and for society becomes all the more vital. A Catholic/Christian culture is part of the glue that holds democracy together. The promotion of rights and responsibilities that underpin that democratic culture is a proper aim of Catholic education.

Catholic education sets high bars. Catholic schools exist to propose the high standards associated with ordinary Christian life to young people. It is seldom, if ever, the case that any single individual within the school, be it the chair of the board of management, the principal, a teacher, or the janitor, has mastered perfection or, indeed, holiness. That reality should not be an excuse to lessen the standard, but rather should serve to incentivise the bearers of the Christian message to be more desirous of living up to it.

**Who wants a Catholic education?**

Some may claim that Catholic education is not what the people in this or that parish really want. But is that true? Average Catholic Christians today are aware that secularism, consumerism, materialism and relativism all have an unhealthy grip on our society, blocking the access of the next generation to truth, beauty and goodness. Pope Francis's identification of the 'disposable' society or 'throwaway culture' in which we live finds a deep echo in the hearts of very many in Western society.

Parents are naturally aware of their primary responsibility as educators but find it hard to educate in such a hostile environment. They are becoming ever more wary of the tech giants who have their own unspoken agendas. They sense a loss of control in society – with stupidities being easily entertained, and a sense that no one is in charge. They have caught horrific glimpses of the dark side of the internet, yet parents find that they cannot even depend on their own state or political structures to protect children from the excesses of online pornography, to mention but one fear.

Parents depend on schools to enrich and supplement whatever education that the busy home can provide, to help young people to see beyond the mundane. While some parents may not be *ad idem* with the Catholic Church on one or more issues, they also know that a good Catholic education is an education in freedom, and that a proper formation in conscience is a very effective help to young people in making good life choices for themselves as they grow older. A Catholic education creates secure individuals who, should they wish and with the help of God's grace, have the capacity to realise their natural and supernatural potential.

So when parents choose a Catholic school, they should get what they have chosen – a school which re-proposes the teachings of Jesus Christ which will redound to the good of the individual, the family, the Church and the whole of society.

That is the focus of this book – to show what Catholic education is, to explain its value, and describe how a school can deliver it. Catholic schools need to be clear on what they want to do and not permit carelessness or inadvertence to result in the short-changing of parents who are looking for the Catholic quality mark.

**The Constitutional position**
Many of the roots of our present education system lie in the 19th century. Over the past three generations the system has largely evolved within the framework of the 1937 Irish Constitution. Articles 41, 42 and 44 of the Constitution are the most directly relevant articles which impinge on education. While not having much to say about schooling per se, the Constitution does speak more about education, and specifically the rights of parents.

So, for example, the Constitution declares that

> The State recognises the family as the natural primary and fundamental unit group of Society, and as a moral institution possessing inalienable and imprescriptible rights, antecedent and superior to all positive law. *(Article 41.1)*

The Constitution then affirms that

> The State acknowledges that the primary and natural educator of the child is the Family and guarantees to respect the inalienable right and duty of parents to provide, according to their means, for the religious and moral, intellectual, physical and social education of their children. *(Article 42.1)*

While requiring in *Article 42* that children receive a 'certain minimum education', parents can provide this education at home or in school, and

> the State shall not oblige parents in violation of their conscience and lawful preference to send their children to schools established by the State, or to any particular type of school designated by the State.

The Constitution does put an onus on the State to provide for free primary education, to supplement and give reasonable aid to private and corporate educational initiative, and provide other educational supports, 'with due regard, however, for the rights of parents, especially in the matter of religious and moral formation.'

The Constitution also, since 2015, specifically recognises the rights of children. Quoting *Article 42A*

> The State recognises and affirms the natural and imprescriptible rights of all children and shall, as far as practicable, by its laws protect and vindicate those rights…

Unfortunately, in international law children's rights can be misused to undermine family rights. But the specific mention in the Constitution of the rights of the family as the primary educator makes it somewhat harder in this country to place an unnatural wedge between children's rights and the duties of parents towards children.

Even a cursory reading of these constitutional articles makes it clear that groups of parents working together, either in parishes or other structures, are welcome to have schools which will provide education within a specific characteristic spirit, such as that provided by Catholicism. To be able to help young people access an education system imbued with two thousand years of knowledge and learning is a wonderful privilege not available to everyone across the globe.

**An urgent reality**

Our western democratic culture is undergoing a major upheaval at the present time, as witnessed through the politics of the cultural clashes across Europe and the US. What are clear fundamental truths, even in the scientific world – that life begins at conception, that biology is not a social construct – are being stood on their heads. The impact of globalisation together with the ubiquity and immediacy of social-media influences have accelerated the rate at which great change can occur. An examination of the major current western worldviews – secular and Catholic-Christian – is needed before we can see what this means for education.

This book, in identifying the sources of our current upheaval and how these are impacting on our education system, will explain how a true Catholic education can serve as a strong personal vaccine for children.

*Endnotes*

**The 2020 Programme for Government** aim is to increase parental choice. 'The Government will continue to expand the plurality of our schools to reflect the full breadth of society.' (see page 96 of *Our Shared Future*)

**Catholic voluntary secondary schools are among the most poorly state-funded school type** – According to the ESRI *Governance and Funding of Second-level Schools in Ireland* (2013) report: 'it is clear that voluntary secondary schools receive a significantly lower proportion of funding from the state and, as a result, are more reliant on voluntary contributions from parents and on general fundraising.'

**Abuse in New Zealand institutions** – see www.rte.ie News, 16 December 2020. This is but one other example. There are many other international reports into institutional abuse which do help to understand the scope of the problem faced. These include eugenics and sterilization campaigns in the United States, Denmark, Finland and Sweden. Stalin's regime in Russia tortured and punished political dissidents, under the guise of mental illness treatment. The Army and CIA in the United States also have histories of testing psychiatric drugs on unwilling patients or soldiers. Abuse that happened in Ireland was neither distinctly Catholic nor distinctly Irish, but is nonetheless inexcusable, especially as trust was invested in entities because they identified as Catholic.

On **Frank Duff's Legion of Mary** the Mother and Baby Homes Report (2021) comments: "before the 1970s, Regina Coeli was the only institution that assisted unmarried mothers to keep their infant". Regina Coeli was a Dublin hostel opened by Frank Duff in the 1930s and run by the Legion of Mary which offered a more humane alternative to the Mother and Baby Homes. Frank Duff strongly believed in the mother/child bond and offered a true, Christian alternative to what was happening elsewhere.

# Chapter 2
# Light and shade – as seen through Catholic eyes

> *Key Takeaways*
>
> *Perennial media hostility to Catholicism seeks to condition Catholics to despise their religious culture.*
>
> *There has been a gradual decline in public worship as well as in the quality of Irish life. This has made it harder to communicate spiritual messages within the school system.*
>
> *On the bright side, young Irish people are among the most religious in Europe, with Catholics involved in many community and charitable undertakings. Many young parents continue to pass on the Catholic faith they have received and want schools to support them in that task.*

**Hostility**

As mentioned in the last chapter, within Irish mainstream media there is a visible under-current of hostility towards Catholicism and, by extension, towards Catholic education.

This is not simply a consequence of the existing widespread distrust that relates to practically all institutions. Some is legitimate hostility towards real failures, especially the abuse scandals and related cover-ups. On top of that there is a viewpoint which unloads most of the faults of our history solely at the door of Catholicism. In addition, there is an attempt to sow suspicion, as if there was something ulterior happening in the provision of Catholic education. This is not solely an Irish phenomenon, as it is happening across the western world. And, perversely, it makes sense. Secularism, as we shall see later, feels it requires a winner-takes-all mentality in the clash of cultures if it is to survive. Unable to co-exist with religious worldviews it thus cannot tolerate any opposition. When one adds to that relentless opposition the lack of robust Catholic voices audible in the public square then secularism advances unchecked.

## Light and shade – as seen through Catholic eyes

A visiting Martian seeking to judge society based Irish mainstream media content will find very few clues that Catholicism had rendered any worthwhile service to society over past centuries. Whatever the evil, the probable cause is our Catholicism. The characteristic spirit of being Catholic is often spoken of as if it were a burden. As a result there is little public kudos to be gained by anyone seeking to defend Catholic schools, be it on admissions policy, academic standards, curriculum content, public service commitment or quality of educational experience, because invariably the matter will be mis-reported.

The media tactic of closing down alternate views is well known and predictable. An issue arises – even something as small as a parent objecting to some school rule with a perceived Catholic angle – and the media pile on, often making false claims. To avoid creating or adding unnecessarily to controversy within the school community, some change may be made by the school which could be seen as acquiescing to media pressure. Often, a school might not comment for much the same reason: controversy is not what schools are about. The view that the general public is left with is that the school was obviously wrong, that Catholics can't be trusted to get it right – and another blow for freedom has been struck by our vigilant media. For Irish media, anti-Catholicism is a smouldering old weed which never burns out, and bullying Catholics always seems to work.

This hostility to Catholicism is part of a wider media narrative which has a poor understanding of history and often appears to have little interest in putting any past mistakes in perspective. And should any historian risk promoting a more nuanced outlook on past history which might seek to redeem Catholicism, then he or she would be inviting opprobrium and even exclusion from academia.

Like the frog which is gradually cooked in the slow-heating saucepan, Catholics are being progressively conditioned into despising their own culture. These reductionist projections of Catholicism both in Ireland and internationally are now being mirrored in attitudes expressed about patriotism across the Western world. Expressions of a proper patriotism (the love of one's country and its symbols) are equated with unwelcome nationalism, with the understanding of what it means to be patriotic being truncated into negative and exclusive nationalistic sentiment, making any declaration of patriotic sentiment uncomfortable or silencing people from expressing love of their country. Without really understanding what has been happening, Irish society has been the victim of an anti-Catholic woke-thinking for over a generation, and this has taken a heavy toll on Catholic enthusiasm.

**Shade**

The Census figures indicate a declining number of Irish people identifying as Catholic. The 2016 Census showed a drop from 82% to 78% over a five-year period. Other indicators suggest that a significant percentage of those do not fully identify with a Catholic way of life. Average weekly Mass attendance across Ireland appears to be around 35%, and under 20% in Dublin, and in some places even lower. The gradual drift of people away from Mass and from the sacraments might suggest that many people now live their lives with little or no reference to belief or trust in God. The degree to which many saw little difference during Covid-19 lockdowns between online worship and the real thing displays a deep misunderstanding of how worship should be conducted. There has also been a drastic decline in family prayer.

Over 67% of Irish people voted in 2018 to remove the constitutional protection provided for unborn life, although many of those may not have realised where that decision would lead after a mere couple of years.

Community engagement across Ireland has declined, with organisations having to work much harder to attract volunteers. At the same time society has become increasingly diverse with community neighbourhoods comprising a wide variety of cultural, religious and non-religious backgrounds, and more in need of positive community engagement than ever.

The messages of the contemporary western culture are to be witnessed everywhere across Europe and Ireland is no exception in that regard: the cult of the celebrity, increasing drug usage, binge drinking, and pornography. Even when things really go off the rails resulting in tragic events such as murders of children by children, or patricide or fratricide, Irish society no longer engages in national soul-searching, nor does it look for solutions beyond the immediate circumstances. It is much easier to accuse individuals of being monsters than it is to reflect more deeply on the environment which has contributed to what they have become. Those working with young people witness increasing depression and mental illness, and as well as the despair and emptiness which is tragically associated with many suicides.

This overall decline feeds into the climate in schools, making it much harder to communicate spiritual messages. Some parents, due to their life circumstances, may feel disaffected from matters of faith. Others may know very little about their faith due to inadequate formation or lack of interest. As with wider society many Catholic teachers have fallen away from regular practice or may lack the confidence or the personal education to deal with the complex moral dilemmas that surface in the classroom regularly. Others lack experience and capacity in negotiating the politically correct culture of our time, with its overtones of swift puritanical and unforgiving judgement on those who step out of line. Many young people rightly feel short-changed in an education system which would appear to be afraid to stand up and explain itself.

The shade is particularly dark when one considers the mistakes of Catholic leaders and institutions of the past. A proper perspective is needed in this matter and hopefully as time passes that will come to be. What comes across clearly however is that the much justified condemnation of past actions centres not on criticism of the Gospel message but on the fact that it was not heeded by individuals and institutions. This should be an encouragement and a reminder to Catholics to commit more readily to living Gospel values and not be lulled into acquiescing to the darker sides of our present culture.

**Light**

Of course, there is another, very different way of looking at all of this.

An overwhelming majority (78%) of Irish people identify as Catholic with a substantial percentage of these displaying an interest in practising their faith. The US-based Pew Research Center found in 2018 that Ireland is Western Europe's third most 'religiously observant' country, with 24% showing 'high levels of religious commitment'. This was measured by looking at 'frequency of attendance at religious services, frequency of prayer, degree of importance of religion in the respondent's life and belief in God.'

A Stephen Bullivant European Social Survey study found that Irish people aged between 16 and 29 years are among the most religious in Europe with 54% of the Irish in this cohort identifying as Catholic – almost half of whom pray weekly, alongside 39% of whom who say they have no religion. While the value of the Mass may not be as appreciated as it should, young people show a great interest in spiritual matters and there are many thriving young Catholic groups countrywide.

According to researcher Gladys Ganiel of Queens University Belfast, writing in August 2018,

> One of the most striking findings of my research was that Irish people could not stop talking about Catholicism. What they told me was that the institutional Church had let them down… Such disillusionment was prompting people to create new spaces where they could practice religion outside or in addition to the institutional Church. For me, these new spaces signalled a type of religious vitality, and demonstrated that Catholicism remains important in some ways, for some people.

At least 33% of Irish people believe that the right to life of all unborn children should be fully protected, despite almost unanimous media suggestions in 2018 that campaigners supporting the retention of the Eight Amendment (i.e. pro-life campaigners) were being thoroughly deceitful. (Even two years after the introduction of abortion absolutely foolhardy canards about pro-life people, such as, for example, one linking pro-life, white nationalism and eugenics, go unchallenged on mainstream media.)

Catholic individuals, as well as people involved in church groups and agencies, do Trojan work in their communities, involving themselves in a wide range of voluntary and professional service provision to the poor and needy. Catholic-inspired charities continue to be household names in Ireland and also all over the developing world.

The increasing diversity in Irish society has invigorated many Catholic and other Christian parishes. Catholic schools and diocesan youth groups have risen to the challenge of the contemporary culture and provide a wide range of services for young people. Many Catholics are active in agencies providing mental health supports to young people.

Many young parents feel privileged in being able to pass on the Catholic faith they have received and want their schools to support them in that task. With the right encouragement such parents are more than willing to play their part in a school that is true to its Catholic ethos.

There is undoubtedly a crisis in our western culture, which is having very negative effects on Irish society. Despite clear mistakes by Catholic individuals and leaders and an unreasonable media hostility, many Irish people rightly see Catholicism as a beacon of hope. A deeper look at our Western culture and at the Catholic-Christian worldview will reveal why that hope is well placed. Catholic schools have an important role to play in sustaining that hope.

*Endnotes*
For **US-based Pew Research Center** see *www.pewresearch.org/fact-tank/2018*
For **European Social Survey study by Stephen Bullivant** see *https://www.stmarys.ac.uk/research/centres/benedict-xvi/docs/2018-mar-europe-young-people-report-eng.pdf*

For **Gladys Ganiel of Queens University Belfast, writing in August 2018** see *https://www.rte.ie/author/986959-gladys-ganiel*

For **canards about pro-life people** see interview by Tom Dunne of *Newstalk* with a reproductive rights activist 28 January 2021 on *www.newstalk.ie*

# SECTION 2
# The difference a God makes

Aguste Comte, a 19th century French philosopher, is best remembered today for his philosophy of positivism and as the founder of sociology – which he regarded as the queen of the sciences.

For Comte, true knowledge came from experience of natural phenomena. Information derived from sensory experience, interpreted through reason and logic, was the only source of all certain knowledge. Anything then that is not verifiable or falsifiable, does not belong to the realm of reason.

So also with nature – for him it was purely functional.

Much of Comte's original positivism continues to underpin western democratic society. Society has been left with a truncated reason based solely on empirical facts and without any God or any notion of transcendence. Right and wrong have no reliable reference, and religion has no place.

Comte's eccentric sociology was found out long ago. Ecology now reveals that nature has something more to say to us after all beyond pure functionality. And as facts are now being replaced by narratives, and new science is in the thrall of political forces, truncated reason is proving itself less than useful.

As the following chapters will show, the secularist positivist worldview does not serve societal needs. Secularism has been successful insofar as it has fed off the Christian roots of democracy, but it has grown more distant from these as the decades have passed. For education, secularism is radically insufficient as it presents a purely functional view and leads to the abandonment of truth in education.

# Chapter 3
# Understanding the Catholic-Christian worldview

> *Key Takeaways*
>
> *Secularism wishes to remove all religious influence from society.*
>
> *Christians are followers of a person – Jesus Christ, who is the Son of God. They believe that God is the creator of all things and that humankind is a special creation of God's.*
>
> *The basic norms for moral behaviour have a universal basis, with Catholics seeing these as our inbuilt instructions for use, part of our human nature. These together with the wisdom shared by Jesus Christ form the Christian moral framework.*
>
> *Christian belief has shaped our world. A purposeful life, the inherent dignity and equality of all, the importance of reason, being planetary stewards, and recognising the significance of justice and charity have always been part of the Christian worldview.*
>
> *For the Catholic-Christian, education of the whole person starts by asking about meaning and purpose.*

Throughout humankind's history there have always been tensions between the temporal and spiritual orders, between the rulers of this world and the spokespersons for the next. At the beginning of our modern democratic age these tensions were addressed by a clear separation of church and state, a separation which was built upon the learning of previous centuries.

Now, over the past two generations, a growing political secularism has steadily sought to redefine the terms of this separation. It is now presented as the need to *remove religion* from society. And once religion is removed, society finds a need to develop its own secular version of religion.

To understand this further, an examination of the Christian outlook on humanity and society is called for which can then be compared and contrasted with the secular perspective. The how and why of the removal of Christianity from the public square is looked at together with the implications of this for Catholic education.

**What does it mean to be Catholic?**

A Christian is a person who believes that Jesus Christ is the Son of God. To become a Christian there is an initiation ceremony – a person is baptised 'in the name of the Father, and of the Son and of the Holy Spirit'. There are more non-Christians than Christians in the world and within Christianity and Catholicism itself there are those for whom their Christian allegiance is partial. Catholic Christians, who see the Pope as their spiritual leader – the vicar, or representative, of Christ on earth – are the majority Christian group.

Religious belief is closely tied with morality. The strong similarity of basic principles of right and wrong – throughout time and across all religions – is not surprising as religions generally have sought to echo the 'ethical intuitions of mankind', and have come up with broadly the same answers to perennial questions. The basic norms for good moral behaviour thus have a universal basis. For Christians, these are understood to be part of our inbuilt instructions for use, or part of our nature as humans, which we can come to know with our reason, and together with the wisdom coming from Jesus Christ form a Christian moral framework. Thus, although this book is written from a Catholic perspective, many of the ideas contained here will have a broader Christian appeal, as well as being of value to those of other religions.

Christians are followers of a person – Jesus Christ, who is the Son of God. They believe that God is the creator of all things and that humankind is a special creation of God's. Soon after its origins, humankind had fallen in some way (the original sin), and God sent his Son, Jesus Christ, into the world to redeem humans from sin, so that after death they could join with Him again, forever, in eternity.

As creatures, made of matter and of spirit, human beings are passing through this world, with their sights set on seeking happiness here in this life and on eternal happiness in the life to come. For Christians, all of creation is somehow caught up in eternal life. This world is important in the here and now, but also as a preparation for that eternity to come.

Christians understand that what really counts is their love for God and their love for all other human beings, who are equally loved by God. Christians are called to love their neighbour, where any and every human person who crosses our path in some way qualifies as a neighbour.

Some of this Christian worldview is shared by other religions. For example, many religions believe in the one God who created all things. Such a belief in God can have a wide-ranging impact on one's view of the value of fellow human beings.

Also, within Christianity itself, there are some variations on matters of faith, which may lead an individual to draw different conclusions on how one should live one's life.

**What Catholic-Christians believe**

It is useful to examine the Christian creed through the lens of modern society, and to see where that belief takes us. Many aspects of the world which are very familiar to us today have been strongly shaped by Christianity. Such significant Christian views are listed below.

- The Christian worldview draws on a natural knowledge of God which it shares with many other religions and to which are added the rich, additional insights provided by the humanity of Jesus Christ, God who becomes man.

- Christians believe that there is a direction to history – and that the world will end sometime, leading to a final judgment. Life is purposeful but is not pre-determined in any way. At the same time there is a divine providence at work in all our lives.

- In the Christian worldview, the human person is not an accident of the cosmos, nor an aggregate of random molecules, but an individual purposeful person created and willed by God. The inherent dignity and equality of the human person as a person derives from that reality.

- God's creation is an inherently good, ordered and intelligible reality which we can affirm, protect and promote as well as explore and gradually understand.

- The human person is social by nature and shares this world with many other persons, whom he or she loves as other children of God. For the Christian, sharing means more than simply tolerating or respecting. It is an acknowledgement that the fruits of the planet are for all humanity for all time. It is an acceptance that any individual claim for autonomy is always circumscribed by corresponding duties and by claims for justice by others.

- Just as it is true for the universe in general, and for our planet, human persons were made with in-built instructions for use. The more humans can discern these instructions and seek to live by them, the better this life will be for individuals and for society. A creator can instil an 'ought' into his creation, which we humans can uncover.

- Human beings have within themselves 'a primal memory of the good and the true', commonly known as conscience, which serves as an internal objective guide to behaviour.

- By becoming man, Jesus Christ has helped us understand our humanity more fully. There is a wisdom deriving from knowing the life of Jesus Christ which can be of benefit to the whole of humanity.

- God, in making us in his image and likeness, endowed human persons with an intellect with which to reason and with a will with which to love. The human person is expected to use these faculties and not neglect their development, abuse them or suspend their use. Reason must rule – especially when our emotions fight for supremacy.

- The requirement to love each other as children of God, that is to love our neighbour, moves beyond a desire for justice for others into the area of charity. Charity is when our giving to the other goes beyond the realm of what the other person is entitled to and it is a fundamental mark of Christian life.

- A follower of Jesus Christ is not a disinterested bystander in life, waiting for the eternal life to come. Rather, the world in which we live is a co-operative adventure between God and us, his unique creatures. He has made us to be co-creators, to help shape the best possible world we can this side of the grave, thus helping prepare all of humanity and the world itself, for the next life.

- For a Christian, education is integral, it is of the whole person, as it is the whole person who makes decisions and who acts in the world – and education starts by asking about meaning and purpose.

### *Endnotes*

**Secularism has been successful insofar as it has fed off the Christian roots** – Tom Holland's *Dominion – The Making of the Western Mind* (Little, Brown 2019) convincingly shows the influence of Christianity across the ages, including on secularism.

**Ethical intuitions of mankind** – See Chapter 5 of D Vincent Twomey (Ignatius Press, 2007) '*Pope Benedict XVI: The Conscience of Our Age*' for a fuller discussion on this.

**What Catholic Christians believe** – a more in-depth background to these beliefs can be found in *Vatican Council II: Gaudium et Spes* – see Chapters 2 and 3.

# Chapter 4
# Secularist worldviews

> ***Key Takeaways***
>
> *Secularism is a philosophy which takes its principles from the material world, ignoring God's existence.*
>
> *An initially healthy Western separation of Church and State has now evolved into a secularism seeking the removal of all religion from the public square.*
>
> *Secularism claims that democracy is rooted in ethical pluralism and that there is no truth. In fact, democracy is grounded on fundamental truths about human nature, truths which Catholic-Christianity protects and upholds.*
>
> *True political dialogue – among other things – rests on citizens believing their religious convictions to be true and from there works towards justice and peace. For this reason Christianity is a better arbiter of the public square than secularism can be.*

## Healthy secularity

Ireland, due to its historical link with the UK and to the important role played by the Catholic Church throughout history in forging Ireland's identity, is a unique tangle of Church and State. Up until around two generations ago, as the new, primarily Catholic, Ireland emerged from under the wing of the United Kingdom, dependence on educated religious leaders in public life might have been understandable, if not at times excusable.

An unfortunate by-product of this early dependency on religious leaders is that clericalism in Irish society still lingers somewhat to this day – that is, a leaning on spiritual leaders to resolve temporal problems, and a lack of socio-political engagement by lay people. A healthy secularity has more recently emerged over the past generation - one which properly leaves it to lay people to resolve the issues confronted by Catholics in our world, while also welcoming the rights of bishops to be genuine pastors to their flocks.

## Unhealthy secularism

Secularism, on the other hand, is a philosophy which seeks to interpret life taking its principles from the material world, to the exclusion of religion. For secularists, God's existence or non-existence is of no consequence in the here and now. As originally envisaged, when, two centuries ago, the new governmental forms of democracy were taking shape, secularist thinking sought the separation of religious institutions from the institutions of the state. This was desirous both for church and state as it left each one to look after their own spheres of influence. Over the centuries, the intermingling between church and state had brought both good and ill to society. Their separation was a helpful and early historical working-out of a new relationship between the democratic state and the churches, reflecting an understanding of how to 'give to Caesar what belongs to Caesar and to God what belongs to God.'

Secularism has further evolved in recent decades giving rise to modern secular liberalism which seeks to restrict any influences of religion on society. Secular liberals advocate the separation of church and state in the formal constitutional and legal sense. They view religious ideas about society as having nothing of real value to offer and thus give these no special status. Further, they argue that attempts to give them status is to impinge on the freedom of others. The more secularised the democracy the more state law will reflect non-religious ethics. So, for example, in recent years the dismantling of structures of the traditional family and of marriage, or the emergence of new understandings of what equality means is the fruit of such liberal secularism. As discussed later in the context of the proposed new primary school curriculum, the Irish state appears no longer happy simply with the idea of separation, since it is effectively proposing a new replacement religion in schools, one that is state-sponsored, one without God.

Secular liberal society wishes to manage without God. Its view is that the more God is kept out of the picture, the better for us all. Christians are free to be Christian as long as they keep it private. Christianity should have no public manifestation. It is expected that if one wishes to involve oneself in political life for example, one should leave one's religion behind. If somehow, a Christian person can become sufficiently purified by disavowals of religious influence, secular society may then seek to accommodate that de-Christianised voice in the public square.

## Religions only cause problems

Some secularist voices argue that by the fact of their plurality, religions are divisive, and for this reason are the cause of wars and divisions in society. They say that one only needs to look at many conflicts in the world today, which are 'caused' by fundamentalist religions. The only solution to this is to remove all religious influence from public life and the public square – essentially making religion a private matter. Secularists are recognisable by the alacrity with which they link fundamentalism to religion – not accepting that all religions, just as with all forms of government, have pathologies which must be avoided. By equating fundamentalism – and thus violence – with religion, secularists provide a potent argument against giving public space to religious views.

Those who criticise violence within Christianity are certainly living in a selective past, a complex past which is not properly a subject of discussion in this book. However, it should not go unsaid that in recent centuries Christians have been at the receiving end of much violence and that for many years now are the group who, worldwide, currently suffers most from persecution on account of their faith.

As for the existence of a plurality of religions, why should that be a problem in this modern age? If a variety of political parties within society is not seen as divisive or a threat to freedom, why should the existence of a variety of religious groups be seen to be?

It was anti-Catholicism in 1950s America, rather than secularism, which pressurised John F. Kennedy to relegate his religious beliefs to the private sphere and to secularise the US presidency. In modern secularism, public manifestations of religion are seen as an infringement on the rights of those who do not share that religion and therefore are to be avoided. This view can be accompanied by a subtle and sophisticated form of prejudice towards religious symbols and a hostility towards believers. A more absolutist secularising position maintains that those who disagree with this secularising view are imposing their religious views on others.

Some of those who oppose the place of religion in the public square claim that democracy is anchored in ethical pluralism, that is, that all outlooks on life are of equal value, that citizens may claim autonomy for any particular choices they make, and that lawmakers should respect that choice. While a believing Christian citizen might have some difficulty in fully accepting this claim, he or she would be quite ready to put competing views into the public square, to help shape a better society. However, secularists are inclined to make an additional claim, seeking to declare any contributions by Christians null and void.

Secularists essentially ask – in the name of tolerance – that people should not base their contribution to society on their own particular understanding of the human person or of the common good. In short, ethical pluralism applies except for those who say that there are boundaries that should be observed. This secular intolerance has the effect of neutralising any contribution to public debate – when such derives from Christian social teaching or a Christian worldview or indeed any other coherent religious worldviews. The claim is also used to neutralise ideas which, though firmly grounded in science, coincide with the Christian solution to particular challenges. This is particularly true when it comes to questions such as, for example, when life begins, the answer to which is one on which the accepted mainstream scientific view and the Catholic view coincide.

While not seeking to personalise the matter the following quote from now President Biden clearly captures the impact of this secularist ideology on those professing Catholicism. In 2020 Mr Biden declared that his faith 'will continue to serve as my anchor, as it has my entire life.' Yet, in speaking to America magazine in 2015, Mr Biden said 'What I am not prepared to do is impose a precise view that is born out of my faith, on other people.' In this he was referring to how he would legislate on abortion. Thus even though science testified to the life of the unborn, as this coincides with his Catholic faith, Mr Biden is not ready to oppose abortion in any way.

**Christianity is needed to control secularism**

It is in this that fundamentalist secularism shows its intolerance. Its view of the world – anchored in an ethical pluralism built on the shifting sands of opinion – wishes the world to accept the notion that there is no truth, and that any group which claims that there is a truth is a threat and therefore must not be allowed space in the public square.

## Secularist worldviews

Those who make such secularist claims are simply not consistent. Tolerance, by their standards, is only for those who hold no conviction with respect to truth.

However, there is a more serious difficulty in ceding to such a secularist world view.

Pluralism is not an absolute. A society of consistent relativists will ultimately become subject to the law of the strongest. On the other hand, true political dialogue presupposes that citizens take their convictions seriously because they believe them to be true. The resultant dialogue leads to a capacity for compromise - making possible a life of peace, freedom and justice. In short, real politics and true democracies come about through the acknowledgement of the rights of individuals to hold particular views.

Thus if society wants a philosophy to referee the public square it should be one which will take the participants seriously in acknowledging and testing their claims to truth. Secularism is certainly a valuable participant in those debates, but it can only be that. A religious outlook which acknowledges the existence of truth and which seeks to find it through the exercise of charity can be a much better arbiter.

### *Endnotes*

**plurality of religions** – before the ironing out of Church-State relationships at the emergence of 18th & 19th century democracies, when the Gospel tenet of 'give to Caesar' became a practical reality, the plurality of Christian denominations was actually a source of much political unrest.

**impact of this secularist ideology** – for more on how secularism shapes the mind of President Biden see Chapter 20 *Escaping the Bunker* by M Hamilton (So What Imprint, 2021)

# Chapter 5
# Contrasting and competing

> ***Key Takeaways***
>
> *Christians know the right way to live by using reason, acknowledging their createdness and allowing the whole person to be part of human decision-making.*
>
> *For secularists, God is irrelevant, and life is about using freedom to maximise personal autonomy, while secondarily acknowledging the needs of others. Societal morality for secularists is anchored in human rights treaties.*
>
> *Secularism seeks to deny religion any space in the public square. Secularism is not neutral as it denies anyone else's claim to objectivity.*
>
> *By denying that there is a human nature, genuine human rights are threatened and democracy is shorn of its Christian-inspired roots.*
>
> *When it comes to education, secularists place no value whatever on those things which are central to the Christian worldview – the fundamental questions of meaning and purpose.*

**In the Christian corner**

In many ways secularism acts as an alternative religion. It is a set of beliefs concerning the cause, nature, and purpose of the universe and contains a moral code on how we humans should conduct our affairs. So when comparing and contrasting the Christian worldview with that of liberal secularism it is helpful to use a sound religious lens in order to understand the differences.

Every religion has its beliefs, and some rules of morality (code) as well as particular religious practices. Catholics/Christians believe in a God who created us and our surroundings, who sent his Son into the world to redeem us, and who is actively involved in his creation. We, his human creatures, are all equal in dignity before Him.

## Contrasting and competing

This God has given us a morality which is 'written on our hearts' and which human beings can know through conscience. We can know the right way of living by using our reason, allowing the whole person to be part of our decision-making process and acknowledging our given nature as children of God. Additionally, by God becoming Man we gather additional insights into humankind and morality. God wishes not only that we seek our own good, but also seek the common good of the entire society.

He has also given us a Church to guide us along the path to the heavenly reward he has laid down, and to provide us with spiritual food for the journey. In summary, Christians know and believe in a God who has shown them a way to live, a way that will serve them well in this life and the life to come.
In the 'Christian corner', so to speak, room must also be made for people of other faiths, or agnostics or atheists who do accept the existence of moral absolutes and/or some sort of objective morality.

## In the secular corner

On the other hand secularists do not accept any views on creation, nor any claim to God's existence. For some, God does not exist. For many others, as they see it, God may or not exist, but the question is irrelevant when evaluating how they should live their lives. For them, this life is primarily about the individual human being using freedom to find one's own way and effectively negotiating contracts with other humans along the way. The common good lies in maximising the good of the individual in achieving personal autonomy – with the concerns of others acknowledged when necessary, but coming a distant second.

Without God and without any absolute right or wrong, there is nowhere to anchor objectivity for morality. So it is up to each individual to sort out one's own morality. At a state level, as humans need rules to co-exist, modern secular society tends to start with rules which derive from human rights treaties.

Initially these treaties, due to their origins, reflected a Christian worldview. That protective Christian effect is now fading. Following on secularist interpretations and obfuscation of language over the past six decades, interpretations of these treaties have now developed a strongly individualistic tone, without regard to the given nature of humankind.

For the secularist, since God effectively does not exist, then there can be no universal truth, and all religions are thus equally untrue. Persons should make the most of this life for themselves, and should depend on their reason to form moral judgements; in the affairs of state they should allow themselves to be guided by evolving ideas of human rights.

If Christianity and secularism were seen simply as two competing religions then everyone would all be better off – each would compete for allegiance, and over time they would win or lose converts to their cause. However, an additional claim that secularism makes for itself is that *it should be the only arbiter of the public square*, making pluralism the king, and seeking to mute the voice of any religion or indeed any philosophy which disputes that claim. Once that claim is widely asserted for secularism, as it is for example through its high priests in the modern media, then it becomes all powerful. It then seeks to manage the education of all those wishing to enter the public square.

**How secularism impacts on society**

Secularists argue that their worldview is a force for good in three ways:

- It protects everybody's freedom of conscience and religion and belief by staying neutral between them.

- It allows the state to focus on governing in this world, applying reason to the best available evidence.

- It can combine with human rights standards as a foundation-stone on which to build liberal democracy. This can, in turn, combat other threats from such ideologies as fascism and totalitarianism and communism and the unregulated free market.

In passing, lest some Catholics have not considered the matter, it is worth addressing each of these claims.

- The neutrality that secularism claims effectively states that all religions are equally erroneous. It claims that this is a neutral stance, whereas it is an agnostic stance with regard to the existence of any moral, non-empirical truth. Rather than actually protecting freedom of religion in the public square it silences religion, requiring it to stay quiet and to make no claims to objectivity. Catholicism on the other hand does not prevent anyone's claims to objectivity – rather it seeks to communicate its values, not impose them. It provides its publicly accessible moral argument in the public square and respects the right of each individual to be true to their own understanding of life, and the right of all equally to participate in that public square.

- Reason alone, understood in the limited secular sense as scientific reason – and sometimes referred to in this book as truncated reason because it ignores our nature – is insufficient to govern the world. As secularists in general do not accept any objective truth they often depend on a consequential type of reasoning – they seek to judge the possible outcomes of some action as the basis for determining whether it should be allowed happen or not. So an action may be allowed happen if for example the known consequences are on balance favourable. But as consequences are always diverse it is impossible to calculate them using a single non-moral scale of measurement – thus it is, in principle, an incoherent method of moral evaluation.

  Also, in practice, one needs look no further than Covid-19 and the inability to predict the path or impact of the disease on humanity – despite all the scientific evidence – to show the complete inadequacy of consequentialism. Not only that, but even scientific facts these days (including on Covid-19) find it difficult to break through the censorship cloak of woke thinking in western society, thus depriving reason of its necessary oxygen supply, that is, 'true' facts. Christianity advocates that wise government use *both* reason *and* our understanding of the person as a purposeful creature of God – i.e. reason and nature – in making all decisions.

- Human rights, as originally envisaged, are the result of human reason, built on a Christian understanding of the person and developed within a Christian worldview. By clinging to human rights standards, secularism is using a system supported by a Christian understanding of the person, but which secularism has since sought to gradually empty of Christian meaning.

  For example, our freedom of speech is an inalienable right, which from a Christian perspective inheres in the person and is not a right as such granted by the state. In recent years, as secularist societal movements have sought to cut rights away from their Christian roots, these can become emptied of meaning. So, it is commonplace now to hear secular liberals seeking to place restrictions on freedom of speech through radical forms of censorship – much like the communists of old. For these liberals, freedom of speech was just a convenience which was useful to democracy until now, but in the face of other newer 'goods' promoted under the title of social justice, this freedom has become expendable. Christians can and do accept reasonable, proportionate purposeful limitations on freedom of speech – what they don't do is to deny that the freedom exists.

As can be seen from that example, human rights are only fully understandable within the Christian worldview in which these originated: without such a basis they become subject to those groups who wield most power. Similar considerations arise in dealing with other freedoms such as freedom of association, of religion or of equality before the law as well as all life and death issues. Despite a declared appreciation of the equality of all humans as its first principle for political action, secularism has then tended to deny any rights to the child in the womb or to 'vulnerable' citizens whose life might be tangentially threatened by euthanasia legislation.

- Despite secularists' claims that human rights systems allow liberal democracies to withstand totalitarianism or communism that simply isn't true. Like secularism, these detestable ideologies are also based on pure reason, and are equally materialistic, and when these threaten democracy the most powerful wins out. So rather than protecting society from these ideologies it prepares the ground for them, by detaching democracy from its Christian roots. Ideologies are strong winds of change which can easily uproot the fragile tree of secular liberal democracy unless it is properly anchored in enduring Christian principles.

**Secularism's impact on education**

When it comes to education, secularists place no value whatever on those things which are central to the Christian worldview – the fundamental questions of meaning and purpose. Secularists live as if God does not exist, whereas for Christians God is the most fundamental reality that shapes everything.

At the end of the day, all this makes a difference to how society is shaped. The secularist fruits, coupled with woke ideology – which are being experienced in our third-level colleges – are far from pleasant. Students who believe that an unborn child is fully human and deserving of protection under the Universal Declaration of Human Rights are liable to be called misogynist extremists or even white nationalists. Holding that the sacrament of matrimony (a religious ceremony) is for a man and a woman is regarded as the stuff of homophobic bigotry. Denying that human biology is a social construct is transphobic. Non-conformist views on euthanasia, stem-cell technology, surrogacy and gender difference are to be shouted down. It is not simply that others oppose these views but now there is no allowance for any debate on such matters.

In recent years in Scotland, just as in Ireland, there has been a steady secularist attack on faith schools, which there are almost exclusively Catholic schools, despite these being high achieving schools in the main. Such schools were originally opposed on the grounds that they exacerbate sectarianism. The attacks then moved to insisting that Catholic schools be forced to give equal status in religious education to non-traditional forms of sexual relationships.

A few years ago the editor of the *Scottish Catholic Observer*, commenting on this wrote:

> Catholic schools were a crucial part of killing off institutional sectarianism by allowing the creation of a Catholic middle class whose economic muscle could not be denied a prominent place in Scottish life. These days, significant numbers of Catholic school pupils are the children of modern immigrants to Scotland, who hope their children can also take advantage of a superior education to secure a brighter future. These parents may be Muslim, Hindu or of no religion at all.

Catholic education is liable to be attacked on any front, simply because it is Catholic. Schools will be accused of being elitist or sectarian or of showing no regard for diversity or denying human rights to their students or of not being democratic enough. And there is no doubt that at times some Catholic schools need to up their game. But often the grounds for the attack are almost irrelevant – the end is the same: to seek to undermine Catholic identity. When mainstream media writers bandy terms such as 'spiritual terrorism' with regard to the Catholic vision it is clear that Catholic education will have to anchor itself well if it is to hold its ground.

***Endnotes***

**High achieving schools in the main:** For example, in a study in the past decade undertaken by the University of Glasgow, 99 school inspection reports were examined. Of these, 51% of Catholic schools received "very good" or "excellent" marks compared with 30% in non-denominational schools. (See Ian Dunn, *'Catholic schools are a force for good in Scotland'* in *The Times*, 24 November, 2016.)

**Editor of the Scottish Catholic Observer***:* Ian Dunn*, see 'Catholic schools are a force for good in Scotland'* in *The Times,* 24 November 2016.

Alex Salmond, as first minister of Scotland also acknowledged the legacy of Catholic schools as far back as in 2008. 'Scotland's diversity is a source of strength, not weakness. For too long, the attitude of some has been, at best, grudging acceptance of Catholic education and, at worst, outright hostility. All faith-based schools play a significant role in helping to shape, inspire and strengthen our young people to learn.' (As reported by Kevin McKenna *'Catholics are again Scotland's oppressed minority'* in *The Guardian* 12 February 2017.)

**Spiritual terrorism** – a reference to Irish Catholicism in the context of 2021 Mother and Baby Homes Report made by F O'Toole, *Irish Times* 19 January 2021.

# Chapter 6
# The impact of the secular outlook on education

> *Key Takeaways*
>
> *Different worldviews give rise to different education systems.*
>
> *Secular materialism sees religion as a threat to freedom and wishes for a functional education system to prepare people for the workplace, the marketplace and for active citizenship, including also the higher things of our material world.*
>
> *Secular relativism wishes to remove categories that have been imposed on society (including those imposed by religion) and is fertile ground for woke thinking.*
>
> *The incompatibilities of secular and Catholic education are often obscured by the manipulation of language.*
>
> *The Christian realises that God exists and that it makes absolutely no sense to live as if he doesn't, or to leave aside the immeasurable educational benefit provided by the knowledge of his existence.*

**Unity in messaging**

The objective in portraying these two distinct worldviews – the Catholic-Christian and the secular – is to describe how these radically differ from each other, although the language used by each worldview may often sound very similar. This confusion of language is sometimes deliberate – learning from advertising tactics which seek to present something new in the safe, comfortable language of the old.

Whereas worldviews can easily overlap, education systems do not have the same luxury lest they should become confused. Part of the success of education lies in its degree of coherence. Once declared, the very idea of a characteristic spirit is that it filters down through all aspects of a school. This is one reason why it is afforded such importance in the 1998 Education Act. There is no such thing as a value-neutral school, so all schools are required to identify and live out a coherent set of core values. Once values are identified it allows parents to make choices so that they can properly address the 'religious, moral, intellectual, physical and social education of their children.' *(Article 42.1 Irish Constitution)*

Young students who receive obviously conflicting messages in the classroom are more likely to be sceptical of all messages – this is never a good way to help students identify the ground on which they stand. They may decide to accept or reject that ground later, but they are then doing so with greater knowledge and understanding of the choices they are making. There is no magic neutral zone in which young people hover until they reach full maturity.

Catholic parents generally want their children to understand the Catholic take on reality, just as they want them to know their family roots, and to appreciate the richness and light of their faith, as well as the shade. What their children do afterwards they can do in full freedom, knowing that this full freedom is what a true Catholic education has empowered them for.

**Alternative world views lead to different educational approaches**

In singling out one important aspect of a Catholic ethos in a school – a topic that will be examined in more detail in the next chapter – one would most likely highlight the idea that education is about an all-round preparation for this life – and for the next. Thus, apart from its academic content, such education would include development in virtue, while depending on the example of educators; and on the transmission of a Christian way of living, which includes a strong sense of service. For a Catholic school it is a matter of practice or expediency, but not a matter of faith, as to whether students of other religions attend it or not, or indeed whether Catholics are in a majority or a minority in the school.

Some or indeed many of these principles may also be embedded in the moral foundations of other schools which are not avowedly Catholic or Christian. But these can then be compromised by a range of other educational ideas or challenges.

The most common countervailing ideas in today's society, which feature primarily in the secular liberal worldview, include the abandoning of a belief in truth as a forming power in education as well as the promotion of a merely functional understanding of education.

## A materialist view of the world

Some educational philosophies are purely materialistic, viewing the universe as entirely material, solely the result of physical causes or just a brute fact. Anything that is not scientifically verifiable or falsifiable, according to this understanding, does not belong to the realm of reason strictly understood. Hence ethics and religion must be assigned to the subjective field.

These philosophies can regard religious views as a threat to the freedom of the individual (as religion, through its moral force, can be viewed as limiting our capacity for action), and therefore require that religion be relegated to the inner sanctum of personal life. They insist on the existence of a supposed secular neutrality, where religion can and should have no influence on wider society.

Such secularism seeks to promote a basic material and social security for everyone, while relegating all other views on human good to the private sphere. With this view, the public expression of any conviction should be limited or prohibited as it is seen to be offensive to people of other convictions. Such a philosophy dominates much of educational discourse in western society, especially in universities, leading to a restriction on freedom of expression and a stifling political correctness. This secular liberalism forms the basis of the new Education in Religious Beliefs (ERB) & Ethics programmes for primary schools, which are discussed later.

This materialist view of the world and its impact on education follow entirely logical steps from its first principles:

- The world is simply physical, leaving no possibility for free will or genuine choice.
- This view insists that there is no 'true' or objectively right or wrong way of living because there is no source for such morality.
- Religious views can limit our capacity for action.
- Thus religious views are a threat to our freedom.
- All religion is then best removed from the public square and restricted to one's inner sanctum.

- A secular neutrality should hold sway, with no allowance for the public expression of religious conviction which could be viewed as offensive to others.
- The ideal education system for this worldview is one which is primarily functional – one that prepares for the workplace, marketplace and for citizenship in a secularised culture.
- As regards education in morality it focuses on the personal autonomy of the individual; it only focuses on wider society insofar as it is impacted by the individual. It does not leave much space for the idea of true charity.

**A relativistic view of the world**

Another more humanistic, secular worldview ignores the existence or otherwise of God and sees the world as having been 'created' and shaped by human beings who impose concepts and categories on it. Such philosophies are, again, invariably relativistic, denying the existence of any objective truth – for which there is no source – about anything, even about the human person. The human person and human society is as malleable as one wishes to make them.

Counter-intuitive as it may seem, this way of thinking can seek to place limits on the free expression of convictions, lest anyone be offended, with the result that only certain 'agreed' views are permissible in the public square, with no thought given to whether these politically correct views are offensive to anyone. Convictions that suggest that there might be an objective truth to which one should defer are particularly unwelcome in this regard.

Again, this outlook on life, when applied to an education system, follows certain logical steps from its first principles:

- All human categories are ultimately imposed on society through education.
- Religions are the main carriers of these imposed categories in our society.
- It is important to remove these imposed categories from our education system to facilitate freedom.
- School systems can be sanitised by removing religion and its influences, and any other categories of imposed thought, such as, for example, views on gender identity or gender difference or on marriage or on the meaning of freedom of expression.
- Education should start at aged 0, otherwise re-education programmes will be required for children entering pre-school. This is a reflection of the fact

that the family can also be an unwelcome transmitter of imposed categories which limit a person's freedom.
- Education then becomes primarily about functionality, about preparation for the next stage – the needs of the economy, and also about personal autonomy.

These are not rarefied educational philosophies or ways of looking at the world. These are outlooks that impact on the ground in many different ways today within the Irish education system.

**Being honest about what Christians want**

If, as Christians believe, Christianity is crucially relevant to a proper understanding of humankind, then it is important that all educational disciplines are looked at from a specifically Christian understanding. Catholic education should provide young people not only with a proper theistic foundation but also provide the tools for a Christian cultural critique on developments in modern society.

For some – Christian or otherwise – especially those who see schools as fulfilling a merely functional educational task which is completed in the university and capitalised on in the marketplace, these philosophical differences don't amount to very much. For others, the differences highlight the very reasons they have committed themselves to the educational task.

And it is not as if all world views are somehow compatible. Sometimes incompatibilities need to be spelt out. A basic axiom of logic and principle of life, without which education makes no sense, is the fundamental principle of non-contradiction. As outlined by Aristotle it asserts 'It is impossible for the same thing to belong and not to belong at the same time to the same thing and in the same respect,' Another Aristotelian variant of this is 'the road to Agora cannot both be the road to Agora and not be the road to Agora at the same time and in the same way.' Or, in today's terms, one cannot be both an (atheistic) Marxist and a Christian. Some differences are real.

The Christian realises that God exists. So it makes absolutely no sense to live as if he doesn't, nor to leave aside the immeasurable educational benefit provided by the knowledge of his existence.

## Use of language

Equality is a word with which all people are familiar. When Christians speak of equality they mean the equal dignity of every person before God. So, as a result, racism – as traditionally understood – is not compatible with such a worldview, nor is mistreatment of the elderly nor of the unborn.

Yet when the word 'equality' is used in the political sense, it now can mean many different things. It can have its 'Christian' meaning; it can have a rational mathematical meaning; it can be used to condemn any hierarchy in society because it undermines equality. It can be used to mean that any income disparity is wrong, because that would be tolerating inequality. It can be used to mean that everyone should have an equal opportunity to do everything. Or even more than that, it can be used to imply the necessity for an equality of outcomes (for example, in education). Or, on the other hand, when the concept of equality causes difficulty when talking about the unborn it is easier to deny that the child in the womb has any rights.

When language can undergo such contortions it can blind one to the true meaning of things. And this is often the political intention. People are now confronted regularly with words such as 'tolerance', 'neutrality', 'racism', 'positive', 'healthy', 'wellbeing', 'homophobia', 'gender', 'inclusivity', 'unity', 'respect' and 'rights' – all of which have multiple meanings, with some of these meanings seemingly changing at will. Such is the educational challenge faced by people wishing to be true to the Christian view of the world. Catholic school leaders need to have coherent Catholic dictionaries available to understand the political language games that are being played and to be able to properly present a Catholic understanding of the world to their students.

## Schools are simply stepping stones

Christians should not be naïve about the power of the culture that young people are required to navigate, especially when they reach college age. Often the Catholic school is the last safe harbour for a young person before embarking on the high seas of life. If the ship is properly equipped and has the appropriate supplies on board then the young person is more able to understand and respond to the squalls and the reefs which will be part of his or her future.

A Catholic education should, at a minimum, serve the person much as a good vaccine does – it is not failsafe, but if given in the proper dose, it has the capacity to help keep unwanted viruses at bay.

### *Endnotes*

**There is no such thing as a value-neutral school** – as referenced in NCCA Consultation Paper on proposed ERB and Ethics curriculum (*McLaughlin, 1994; Kieran, 2015; O'Connell, 2015*)

**It is impossible for the same thing to belong and not to belong at the same time to the same thing and in the same respect** - see Aristotle's *Metaphysics* IV 3 1005b 19–20). Another variant of this used by Aristotle is 'opposite assertions cannot be true at the same time' - see *Metaphysics* IV 6 1011b 13–20.

# SECTION 3
# The added value of Catholicism

The gaps in the secularist worldview are plain to see. It cannot fully answer simple questions such as why one should sacrifice oneself now for the future of our planet. Nor indeed more pressing ones such as whether humanity should conduct AI (artificial intelligence) warfare nor why humans should never create test-tube humans. It is an insufficient culture in which to anchor laws and its powerlessness has been shown in the face of the wave of woke thinking sweeping across western society.

The Catholic-Christian worldview provides a more complete view of the human person. It is a view that is more in touch with the reality of humanity, and more likely to provide answers and to lead to a better world which respects the common good.

Armed with an understanding of the Christian worldview it becomes possible to appreciate what Christianity contributes to society, as well as seeing how a holistic Catholic education can prepare a young person for life and not simply for the workplace. This then raises the question: what are the elements that form the basis of a Catholic ethos in schools, and how can Catholic schools live up to their promise?

# Chapter 7

# What Catholic-Christianity contributes to modern society

> *Key Takeaways*
>
> *Catholicism has played a major role in all that is good in modern society, setting standards for democracies, yet Irish Catholics appear to have an inferiority complex about their faith.*
>
> *The Christian insistence on charity has led to an increasingly just world.*
>
> *Catholicism recognises objective truth, promote moral solutions, defends human rights, understands the common good and promotes charity.*
>
> *The principles of freedom that underpin democracy are now threatened by secular liberalism. Catholic education is required to help stem that existential threat.*

## A proud legacy

Western society is rightly proud of our modern civilisation. That billions of people, despite many deep tensions in society, can live with a high degree of harmony and peace is a testimony to the strengths of liberal democracies. Christianity has played a major role in providing the foundation for this civilisation and, despite the past half-century of secularism, continues to underpin much of what is good in modern society. There are also many threats at the door of democracy, which can only be effectively countered by continuing to acknowledge the important elements in its Christian roots.

Despite that largely positive religious contribution, many Irish Catholics appear to have an inferiority complex in the face of aggressive secularism. It has not been helped by a heightened awareness of the failures of Catholics in the past, failures that secularists never tire of pointing out. Catholics have been led, or cowed, into believing that the living out of their faith and the public espousal of Catholic values is somehow an imposition on society.

Fundamentally this indicates a lack of appreciation of the Catholic faith itself. Catholicism helps to make people aware of failings, to honestly admit them, and understand them, without being defeated or disheartened by them. Catholics should understand the reality of sin and sinfulness, and the weakness of will and pervasive ignorance due to sin, which makes it so hard to live up the standards of Catholic faith and morality. Part of the value of a good Catholic education is its ability to help Catholics, and others, understand fairly and honestly the sins of the past, and, indeed, one's own sins, whilst still believing in God's mercy and grace, which give us hope and inspiration, and challenge and empower us to be better in the future.

For those seeking reassurance of what Catholicism has to offer society we briefly review the contribution that Christianity currently makes.

**How Christianity contributes to our political culture**

Earlier some key characteristics of what it means to be a Christian were outlined. In summary, Christians are followers of a person – Jesus Christ, who is the Son of God. They believe in a God who is the creator of all things, and that humankind is a special creation of God's – it being the ultimate purpose of the overall creation. At its origins, humankind had fallen in some way (the original sin), and God sent his Son, Jesus Christ, into the world to redeem humans from sin, so that after death they can join with Him again, forever, in eternity.

Christianity, then, can be viewed in a cultural sense, as a way of life, comprising the outcome of the lived lives of many Christians. It does not propose any given set of laws for society, rather it espouses religious and philosophical principles by which laws can be shaped. It is also true that some of those principles, for example, laws against fraud or murder, do translate directly into what are seen as essential laws.

Liberal democracies are but one – albeit very successful – way in which Christian principles help humanity flourish. Christianity is transmitted throughout the generations, under the auspices of Christ's Church which Christians have been promised 'will last until the end of the age'. Christian educational institutions also assist in transmitting the Christian worldview through time.

The strength of this culture should not be underestimated. Christian culture helps form the habits of hearts and minds, lessens selfish tendencies, and creates trustworthy citizens, thereby setting standards by which our democracies and our markets can operate in freedom.

Our modern democratic state has essentially emerged in the cradle of Christianity, a Christian plant at home in Christian soil. The Christian worldview and its Judaic roots, in conjunction with other influences such as classical Greek philosophy and Roman law undergirds the success that we witness today. Certainly there are many moral outlooks which are espoused by Christianity and which are also promoted by other world religions – something that is not surprising given that the moral law is 'written on our hearts.' But the Christian input to democracy cannot simply be reduced to a moral contribution.

Liberal democracy may not lie at the peak of civilisation, and recent encyclicals focussing on Catholic social teaching have valuable suggestions for the betterment of society, but Christians should be rightly proud than society has got this far. Even that simple hope of improvement derives fundamentally from a Christian idea that history is linear, that there is a forward path and that it is not pre-determined, thus inspiring people to seek to improve the lot of humankind, helping them realise that their efforts count. Life is not an endless cycle on some wheel of fortune for individuals or for society, but rather is shaped by the outcome of our efforts. So the attempts that democracies make to improve the lot of their people, to transform society for the better, rather than just accepting things as they are, are a partial fruit of the Christian outlook.

The Christian sense of the fellowship of humanity and of the equality of all persons before God has contributed greatly to the democratic freedoms that are held in high honour today. The Christian view of the innate value of every human person has acted as a counterpoint to inhuman ideologies, especially during the 20th century. It has helped anchor human rights and the modern concept of individual freedom, as exemplified in the Universal Declaration of Human Rights (1948).

The Christian understanding of freedom and the promotion of the principle of subsidiarity provides a bulwark for the individual against the excesses of any state. The Christian support for private property and the responsibilities arising from it underpin the market economy. The Christian insistence on charity has led to our modern education, health, and welfare systems. The

Christian view on the intelligibility of creation has led to the advancement of modern science, which in turn has been the driver of economic development and human progress over the past three centuries.

**Democracy and the free market needs Christianity**

Democracy is a cultivated plant, not a weed, and so requires well-prepared soil. For strong democratic roots to grow there is a requirement for a Christian formation in ideas such as justice, freedom, the consent of the public to be governed, the limited role of the state, and the role of the church as a voluntary institution. Church/state tensions in Europe over almost two millennia seem to have been a catalyst in helping the emerging 19th-century democratic state to establish an appropriate and workable balance between the state and different religions.

Free-market economies also have prior requirements – trust, being one such example. When trust disappears from the market, as experienced in the 2008 crash, the market can easily collapse. Where corruption is endemic, it is not possible to establish normal and proper trading conditions. Honesty is a key part of a Christian moral outlook.

**Recognising truth**

Christians recognise that it is the nature of the human person to seek the truth, about oneself, about others, and about God. They realise that there is an objective truth, accessible to reason - which when followed, truly frees man.

Our modern secular culture thinks differently. In rejecting God it rejects the possibility of truth. Relativism – the doctrine that truth is not absolute and that morality and truth exist only in relation to culture, society, or in a historical context – acts as the secular culture's religion. It thus opposes any claim to truth.

Yet recognition of truth is essential if the state is to be able to acknowledge the pre-existing truths which have made it possible to have the state in the first place! These truths – such as for example, the inalienable right to free expression – should not be subject to consensus or to the vote of the simple majority. (That is not to claim that this freedom is not bounded by other freedoms and duties.) To that end, many state constitutions were promulgated declaring certain truths to be self-evident and certain rights to be inalienable and inviolable. Times arise in the life of every state when a reminder about such truths is essential if justice is to be served.

**Christianity promotes morality**

One of the roles that any religion carries out in society is the promotion of a public moral culture.

While not espousing particular solutions to everyday political challenges, Christianity requires that Christians never do evil that good may come. It presents values to the individual by way of awakening his or her conscience. In encouraging individuals to do good and avoid evil, Christianity provides the foundation for the ethos or morality of a society, which is a prerequisite to peace and order.

Christianity stresses the inalienable dignity of the human person and the need for people to live their lives so as to contribute to the common good. It promotes the principle of the free association of people and the requirement that decision-making powers be distributed as far as practicable amongst all, commensurate with the common good. Christianity recognises that a free and virtuous society depends on a deeper level of relationships than mere contracts between persons, and thus promotes the principle of solidarity or civic friendship. In this ongoing way, Christianity helps strengthen the seeds of democracy - once these have been successfully sown.

Understanding that humans do not live in an irrational or meaningless world, Christians see a moral logic built into human life, reflecting our connection with our Creator. Therefore, Christians, rather than adding anything to our nature, are simply uncovering the values and norms built into humanity – reading the book of nature, so to speak. This logic is accessible to non-religiously-informed reason.

**Christianity defends human rights**

Thus, there are values which derive from our human essence and which are *inviolable* to everyone who is human. These unconditional values include an understanding that it is never right to kill innocent persons, that human life is inviolable, that all human beings are equal in dignity, and that all human beings have freedom of thought and belief. These values inhere in humanity, and Christianity has helped reveal them to us.

In recent decades, secularism has sought to unmoor these human rights from their origins, by focussing on the autonomous individual to the neglect the common good. A minor – but topical – telling example of this in our modern society is how many feel coerced into a public acceptance of the subjective claims of individuals with whom they disagree. No longer are we expected to tolerate others but there is a requirement (enforced through penalties, sometimes including a loss of livelihood) to 'respect' others, where the evolving interpretation of the word 'respect' is in the hands of those who make the rules. Similarly, the emphasis on personal autonomy in law has turned the traditional (and Christian) understanding of rights on its head – the idea of personal autonomy (especially when coupled with emotional rhetoric) pays little regard to the common good of society and often serves as a charter for selfishness.

In the words of Pope Benedict:

> Individual rights, when detached from a framework of duties which grants them their full meaning, can run wild, leading to an escalation of demands which is effectively unlimited and indiscriminate. An overemphasis on rights leads to a disregard for duties. Duties set a limit on rights because they point to the anthropological and ethical framework of which rights are a part, in this way ensuring that they do not become licence. Duties thereby reinforce rights and call for their defence and promotion as a task to be undertaken in the service of the common good.

## Charity cannot be forgotten

As creatures, made of matter and of spirit, we human beings are passing through this world, with our sights set on seeking happiness here and on eternal happiness in the life to come. All of creation is somehow caught up in eternal life. This world is important as a preparation for that eternity to come. To use a sporting metaphor, a Christian understands this world to be a training ground, where what one does matters because it determines what will happen later on the main pitch. All players have an invitation, even if, as of yet, they don't all play for the team.

Christians understand that what really counts is their love for God and their love for all other human beings, who are equally loved by God. Christians are called to love their neighbour, where every human person in some way qualifies as a neighbour.

Following the example of their founder, the earliest Christian communities dedicated themselves to the poor, to the needy, to orphans and widows. The contrast between Christians and Romans at that time could hardly be greater. For the Romans – and for most pagan civilisations – cruelty, extreme inequality and slavery – were second nature. They were simply unquestioned realities – it was just the way things were. The concept of compassion for the weak was relatively unknown. The very fact that our culture today seeks to encourage compassion, equality and fairness is precisely because of the revolutionary nature of the Christian worldview.

The Church's healing and education mission throughout the ages adapted to the needs of the time. Groups of Christians dedicated themselves to healing with monasteries and fledging hospitals from the 4th century, to university education from the 11th century – and to mass education from the 17th century.

Currently, the Catholic Church is the world's largest healthcare provider. Whereas now in many liberal democracies state systems have taken over the financing and provision of healthcare and education, these state systems were largely built on that original commitment of Christians to caring.

It was the Catholic insistence on caring – on acknowledging the eternal dignity of fellow human beings – that led to people growing in a sense of justice and thus ultimately to state authorities responding to those cries of justice. This continues to this day with Catholic and other Christian charities continuing to respond to societal needs – in areas of intellectual disability or AIDS clinics or homeless supports or addiction centres – these charitable services being forerunners to the state taking more responsibility for its marginalised.

This caring approach is so fundamentally different, for example, from the emerging modern woke culture – there is a rigid dichotomy between charity and woke culture's inability to even listen to different viewpoints.

## This cannot happen without Catholic education

The continued success of our democratic society requires that the principles of Christianity re-inform liberal democracy in order to save it. Over the past fifty years an advancing secular liberalism has been gradually undoing the gains of liberal democracy. The principles of the Christian worldview need to be continually brought to bear on policies and institutions, thus infusing society with a genuine wealth of wisdom which can lead to greater justice, peace and prosperity. This requires Christians who understand what it means to be a coherent Christian, and who can bring upright human and moral standards to bear in the political arena. In turn this requires a robust Catholic-Christian education system.

## The challenges to democracy

The worldwide response to the Covid-19 crisis once again confirmed that the future is a strange land which no one has ever visited. As the virus began to take hold of the world its impact made itself visible in a whole variety of ways, raising questions about health-care, personal freedoms, the right to economic activity and the role of the state.

In a rather similar way we can observe the influence over time that secular liberalism has had on modern society.

For forty years now, various Popes have used the vivid term 'culture of death' to refer to western society's abandonment of principles on the dignity of human life. This highly dramatized term has now become a more appropriate appellation of western society than ever before. Claims of personal autonomy have now created the circumstance where parliamentary democracies pass laws allowing children under twelve years to be euthanised (as for example in Belgium). Demands now for the provision of euthanasia and assisted suicide in many countries may prove insatiable despite the negative impact such legislation has on the quality of life of the weak and vulnerable. Just as within a generation of the legalising of abortion under strict circumstances, an abortion pill was readily accessible to twelve year olds or for use in ones' home, it would not be surprising to find that a poison pill for euthanasia will become similarly almost ubiquitous, including in the hands of either bored or thrill-seeking teenagers.

This abandonment of principles by secular liberalism as witnessed to by the 'culture of death' is now extending to other principles that underpin democracy. This is evidenced by what is happening in liberal American society at present with regard to restrictions on freedom of expression, belief and assembly, all in the name of social justice.

Without a proper understanding of the inalienable right of free expression – something clearly expressed in the Catholic vision – there can be impulse to control the speech – and actions – of those who disagree with the mainstream. A society in which the drive for social justice partitions people into opposing groups, and requires that people perceived as oppressors not be allowed into the public square, and denies any possibility of reconciliation between groups, and foresees violence between such groups, is one which does not recognise the inherent human dignity of every human being, does not understand forgiveness nor charity, and is one in which the delivery of justice is impossible.

Thus, there are real threats to democracy which can only be warded off by the Christian values which underpin it. Ideas of freedom and justice that are close to every upright democrat's heart can become irredeemably distorted when emptied of their meaning by the secular worldview. Democracy needs Christianity more than ever to sustain it.

### Endnotes

**'will last until the end of the age'** – *St Matthews Gospel, Chapter 28, v 20*

**'written on our hearts'** – *St Paul's Letter to the Romans Chapter 2, v 15* (New Testament)

For recent encyclicals focussing on **Catholic social teaching** – see *Compendium of the Social Teaching of the Church* available on www.vatican.va

**Christianity promotes morality** – to understand the contrast between Christianity and the Greek/Roman world in which it flourished cf. Rodney Stark, *The Rise of Christianity*.

**'individual rights, when detached from a framework of duties which grants them their full meaning** - See Pope Benedict XVI, *Charity in Truth, [Caritas in Veritate]*, no. 43)

**'culture of death'** -see *Evangelium Vitae*, translated as *The Gospel of Life*, by Pope John Paul II, 1995. 'Choices once unanimously considered criminal and rejected by the common moral sense are gradually becoming socially acceptable,' the Pope said.

**allowing children under twelve years to be euthanised (as in Belgium)** – In a number of European countries mentally ill and disabled people are killed in hospitals at their request. In Belgium, in 2014, the law was extended to include even children. In the Netherlands (2020) the law was extended to include terminally-ill children aged between one and twelve. In cases of euthanasia some bodies are harvested — with the success of the procedures written up in organ-transplant medical journals. A Canadian newspaper (see *ottawacitizen.com* 6 Jan 2020) says 'Ontarians who opt for medically assisted deaths (MAiD) are increasingly saving or improving other people's lives by also including organ and tissue donation as part of their final wishes.'

# Chapter 8
# How Catholic education prepares a student for life

> *Key Takeaways*
>
> *Catholicism imbues human life with meaning in contrast with a barren secularist outlook which 'robs people of their greatness'.*
>
> *Seeking truth and distinguishing right from wrong are driving forces in Catholic education.*
>
> *The Catholic promotion of virtue helps form the basis of a stable society.*
>
> *Catholic education plays a role in helping people develop a relationship of love with God.*

The dismal future society envisaged at the end of the previous chapter can easily become a worldwide phenomenon, due to globalisation and to the ease of social-media communications. But it is not inevitable. Christianity in the past has shown that it has a powerful capacity to produce witnesses to the truth of things, who in turn can influence change due to humankind's desire for truth. Catholic-Christian education systems are thereby important: these help young people understand the true foundations of life and educate the future citizens who can provide solutions that the world needs. Education within a Catholic tradition best prepares citizens for our modern world.

## Providing meaning and value

Christianity – with its belief in a God who engages with his creation – fills our lives and our world with meaning. It provides people with a sense of purpose in their lives. This contrasts greatly with a barren secularist outlook which – in Pope Benedict's words – by 'robbing people of their greatness', can engender real boredom with life, thus encouraging people to disengage and drop out of society. If life is only about the here and now, then why bother to make any effort? A created and loved person has more to look forward to than someone who may view themselves as an accidental random bunch of cells. Christian education presents a more exciting message as to the eternal value of the here and now – that the present we experience is something that can be shaped into a future.

Christianity also directly helps one establish the value of the other person, as Christians are taught to see others as if it were themselves, and to see the face of Christ in others, especially in those who are in need. Christian education is then, by definition, a formation in tolerance – an understanding of others, even should one disagree with every viewpoint held by the other person. Inclusiveness is a natural consequence of a religion which places real value on the other person.

Ignoring religions, as secularism does, or insisting that these hide away or keep to themselves, means never coming to understand these religions, never being able to distinguish their pathologies should these arise – thus always being unable to address them – and ultimately approaching religions as a threat rather than as a liberation. Christianity, by informing its members in a religious spirit, does help them to understand other religions better.

In learning to value other people, Christians become well formed in the need for justice in society: that is, to give each person what he or she is due. Christian education goes an additional step by promoting charity – practising generosity towards others – which, in turn, increases an awareness among beneficiaries of the need for justice and so drives that forward, making it more likely that the modern state will not ignore or forget those in need, or those who fall through the cracks in even the most efficient of societies. Christian education not only seeks to understand and promote equality but it also seeks that it not be separated from the full recognition of human dignity. The Christian charitable efforts to promote primary and secondary education in many countries across the globe or to promote various forms of health-care has resulted in people seeing these as rights in justice, leading many states to ultimately respond and provide for these rights.

**Seeking truth**

Knowing that God exists, the Christian education tradition encourages the search for objective truth, be it in science, ecology, law or morality. This allegiance to truth is an antidote to the seeking of power, or to the anchoring of all rights in the majority principle.

Closely linked to truth is an understanding of what is right or wrong and the shaping of law. Catholicism, while proposing a moral way of life for its followers, has never proposed a revealed law for society but rather has pointed to reason and nature as sources for law and to the harmony which exists between objective and subjective reason. A Catholic education includes a formation in understanding the existence of right and wrong, in the value in doing the right thing, in the idea of conscience – thus leading the way to providing moral foundations for life, for the democratic state and for our economic and legal systems.

Importantly for our present age, Christianity values reason. Additionally it understands that reason has limitations in shaping society, for moral decisions depend also on the nature of the created human person. By not acknowledging the given nature of created human persons, the secular state struggles to advance principled positions based on moral truths. It operates on a reduced diet, a truncated form of reason – one which draws only on scientific reason. Thus in seeking to answer questions such as whether to conduct experiments on humans or engage in AI warfare, the secular state tries to measure the consequences of such potential actions in coming to a conclusion about them, rather than also looking for answers, say, in the nature of the human person. As humankind has been reminded, this time by Covid-19, the unpredictable nature of the future leaves such consequentialism totally inadequate in guiding decision-making.

The Christian learns the place of reason in his or her own decision-making. For the Christian every action is an action of the whole person and thus an essential element of Christian education is that it be integral, beginning with the meaning and purpose of life. A truly Christian education enables individuals to establish an appropriate balance between emotions, feelings and reason in their decision-making, with due regard to memory and history.

**Learning and living good habits**

The Christian understanding of the human person and of human weakness leads Christian education along the classical path of formation in virtues. Catholic tradition has always promoted virtues as providing the basis for good moral actions whereas secular systems of education, due to a lack of an allegiance to objective good and being underpinned only by a non-directive mentality, shy away from endorsing virtue . The living out of personal virtue forms the basis of a stable society: performing good quality work or being committed to one's family are keys to keeping society ticking over.

This commitment to the promotion of virtue also helps Christians establish the proper traits for leadership in society and moors leadership to virtue rather than popularity or a desire for success. By understanding what constitutes a good person, Christian education is in a position to propose that ideal to people. Given its basic tenets it is arguable whether true secularism can wholeheartedly commit to any specific understanding as to what a good person is, and consequently what a good leader is.

**Recognising the power of knowledge and love**

A Catholic education, in its holistic approach to the person and to knowledge, is all that one would wish for in education in these times. It understands that no education system is value-free: even the choice of subjects offered indicates an understanding of value. It educates, guided by a Christian worldview which has produced enormous fruits for humankind. It has a sense of the unity of knowledge, and realises that this unity links back to a created reality. Its commitment to a comprehensive view of truth requires that the teaching of religion, which plays a unifying role, be highly valued.

Some of these principles may also form part of the moral foundations of institutions which are not avowedly Catholic or Christian – but which can often be compromised or undermined by a range of other educational ideas. As mentioned earlier, the most common of these countervailing ideas are the abandoning of a belief in truth as a forming power in education and the promotion of a merely functional understanding of education.

Catholics recognise that our relationship with God is not merely an intellectual one, but is one that is premised on a relationship of love. Thus the promotion of prayer and spiritual growth also plays an important part in Catholic education and in the shaping of a more caring world.

***Endnotes***

**'robbing people of their greatness'** see Cardinal Ratzinger, '*Church, Ecumenism and Politics*' page 206 (Ignatius Press 2008). According to world-renowned intellectual, Jordan Peterson, the crisis facing young men in particular in western society is ultimately one of not understanding the call to take responsibility wherein one finds life's meaning. This chimes with the Christian worldview.

# Chapter 9
# What constitutes a Catholic ethos in schooling?

> *Key Takeaways*
>
> *God's existence gives key insights into who human beings are and into what this world and the next world are about. It is a key foundation stone for education. For the Catholic, secular realities are important and they are underpinned by eternal realities.*
>
> *A Catholic ethos is brought about through allegiance to objective truth, the pursuit of scholarship and education, and through an experience of all-in service.*
>
> *The truths of faith and of reason cannot contradict each other.*
>
> *Catholic schools should not only be centres of excellence and learning but are also places of faith.*

It is one thing to propose Catholic education as a great gift to the individual and to society: it then falls to individual Catholic schools to deliver on that promise. So, before looking at practical ways in which Catholic education is imparted, it might help to have a living sense of what 'being Catholic' means to an educational institution.

**Characteristic spirit**

While visiting the US in 2008 Pope Benedict had this to say to Catholic educators:

> Every Catholic educational institution is a place to encounter the living God who in Jesus Christ reveals his transforming love and truth. This relationship elicits a desire to grow in the knowledge and understanding of Christ and his teaching. In this way those who meet him are drawn by the very power of the Gospel to lead a new life characterized by all that is beautiful, good,

and true; a life of Christian witness nurtured and strengthened within the community of our Lord's disciples, the Church.

Although somewhat theological in content, this message can be distilled down into a few key ideas:

- Being a Christian is the encounter with 'an event, a person, which gives life a new horizon and a decisive direction'
- Schools are places where staff and students get to know Christ through *truth* and *love*
- That knowledge can be transformative and performative.

Some who consider themselves as having a more real-world outlook of what a school is about may see it primarily as a means of education in key subjects and skills, preparing young people so that they can get on with living life. While not dismissive of the preparation needed for the next life, such practical types see the Catholic input primarily in a religious context – academics are for here and now, religion is to help us with the after-life.

Thus, they might view the desires expressed above by Pope Benedict as a little over the top. Yet such a practical approach, while common, entirely misses the purpose and value of Catholic education. It betrays a clerical view of the world, misunderstanding the place of religion, and is a view likely to lead to the sort of mistakes made in Ireland's past when religion was seen as other-worldly and not part of the solution of how to live this present life well.

The existence of the Christian God changes everything. In particular, it gives deep insights into who we humans are as persons, and into what this world – and also the next world – are all about. A Catholic school educates young people within that context for the here and now – it draws on the wisdom that Christ has revealed. These persons are then well placed to better understand the skills required to 'get on with living this life'.

A secular education works on the assumption that God's existence has no bearing on our lives, and so, effectively, it pretends he doesn't exist. The removal of such a fundamental foundation stone from a system which desires to educate makes no sense.

## What constitutes a Catholic ethos in schooling?

Catholic education also recognises that, ultimately, faith is a personal encounter, so it educates in freedom, leading to Catholic schools being a popular choice for very many non-Catholic families. A good Catholic education presents God, making it possible for the individual to find him and to ultimately personally decide on how to respond, or not, to him.

Nonetheless, the validity of the point expressed earlier by Mr Real World should not be overlooked. Acknowledging the reality of God's existence and how that imbues education with meaning should not take away from the secular nature of much of the content of education. Our day-to-day world is secular, that is, many happenings have no direct immediate connection with religious matters. Yet, underpinning all these events are the religious realities of our existence.

On most occasions when one visits a medical doctor one will draw on his or her years of learning and expertise. One might at times wish to additionally encounter a sense of Christian charity, especially should one's ailments suggest something terminal. Similarly, many practical daily needs are provided for in the local convenience store, but smiling encouragement or a brief interaction with the shopkeeper on matters of local or mutual concerns can turn these events into real encounters between people as persons and not simply as isolated individuals. The normal issues that scientists or lawyers or business people are regularly confronted with are not just questions of how, but rather of what is the right thing to do. Such it is with all our secular spaces – they are underpinned by eternal realities.

Catholic schools are practical spaces where the business of this world, a good secularity, is examined and understood, where the seeds of potential solutions to future societal problems are germinated, and where humankind is helped to view life through the lens of eternity.

**Living out that spirit**

How is that spirit achieved in Catholic schools? Well, by pursuing the goals of scholarship and education, by an allegiance to objective truth, and through providing an experience of an all-in service of the person and of the community.

Looking to the each person's future – a future full of personal demands and struggles – seeking to survive in a society which is replete with uncertainty and moral confusion, and one in which an avalanche of knowledge counter-intuitively leads many people to know even less than they should – a Catholic education is education in hope, not only for the person but for the whole of society.

Day-to-day life is as much about interpersonal engagement as it is about professional competence; thus education cannot be reduced to the three Rs. When it comes to matters of religious knowledge, Catholic schools must also avoid a similar reductionism – course content is not solely a matter of orthodoxy or of learning religious facts. Much more is required: all aspects of a learning community should reflect a life of faith. In the words of Pope Benedict education in faith 'nurtures the soul of a nation'.

Occasionally, the suggestion is made that religion in a Catholic school can be confined to a period in the timetable. Even further, curriculum authorities seem to think that courses which contradict and undermine the Catholic insight into reality can be satisfactorily incorporated into a Catholic school curriculum. These views show an inadequate understanding of Catholic belief. Such a lack of understanding by education authorities is often inexcusable. If one can understand or appreciate a secularist worldview which ignores God's existence, it cannot be all that difficult to understand a worldview which fully acknowledges it.

**Education in truth**

This brings us to the heart of how Catholic schools can best serve their students and ultimately assist society – by educating in truth. The truths of faith and of reason never contradict one another. Catholic schools speak of, and seek to teach objective truth, a truth which encourages a full exploration of the sciences and the humanities, a truth which leads one to understand the difference between right and wrong, and one which leads us to fully understand the role of the human person in relation to others.

To quote at greater length from Pope Benedict's informative address to Catholic educators in the US:

The Church's mission, in fact, involves her in humanity's struggle to arrive at truth. In articulating revealed truth she serves all members of society by purifying reason, ensuring that it remains open to the consideration of ultimate truths.

Drawing upon divine wisdom, she sheds light on the foundation of human morality and ethics, and reminds all groups in society that it is not praxis that creates truth but truth that should serve as the basis of praxis. Far from undermining the tolerance of legitimate diversity, such a contribution illuminates the very truth which makes consensus attainable, and helps to keep public debate rational, honest and accountable.

Similarly the Church never tires of upholding the essential moral categories of right and wrong, without which hope could only wither, giving way to cold pragmatic calculations of utility which render the person little more than a pawn on some ideological chess board.

**Education in faith**

And into all that mix of educational experience comes the more specific requirement of education in faith.

As part of a consultation process around the divestment of a Catholic primary school in North Dublin in 2019, some local Catholic schools who wished to maintain their Catholic patronage, consulted with their parents. While confirming that a change in patronage would have a major effect on the *spirit*, *management* and *culture* of their school the survey forms were dominated by a list of practical effects of the loss of ethos. This included, first and foremost, that the school would not prepare students for the sacraments of Communion and Confirmation. Then followed some likely cultural impacts: that no activity or celebrations which would have a specifically Catholic focus could take place; that there could be no religious references in play, in song or in dance; and the specific relationship between the Irish language and culture and the Christian faith would be undermined. Some of these cultural impacts of a school ethos are certainly more tangible but they are only the icing on the cake of a deeper mission of schools: an education in truth, in love and in Catholic mission.

## Our School is Catholic

Archbishop Eamon Martin in speaking to a group of Catholic educators in Belfast in 2014 said:

> At times we can present our faith as if it were simply a collection of guidelines, rules, rituals and routines, symbols, structures and historical characters. Of course it includes all of these. But if we reduce it to these entirely and neglect the 'spark of faith' and that personal encounter with the love of God in Jesus, then we will end up with something 'worn out' and joyless.

He added that

> our schools are distinctive – they are not only centres of excellence and learning, but they are also places of faith. Thus they should facilitate young people in grasping the truths of faith, growing in love of God and neighbour, and in becoming witnesses for Christ.

To help carry out that mission brings a requirement that students receive instruction in Catholic doctrine and practice at age-appropriate levels, that their sacramental and prayer life is nourished, that they are helped to be more appreciative of the gift of faith, and that witness is given by the school community to a harmony between faith, life and culture. In the words of Pope Francis

> Catholic schools, which always strive to join their work of education with the explicit proclamation of the Gospel, are a most valuable resource for the evangelization of culture.

Undoubtedly such thoroughness or perfection is not easily achievable. The failures of Catholics and/or Catholic schools and institutions in the past have been well publicised, partly because they were rightly held to a higher standard. Such failures often reflected the failure of the wider culture of the time. There may also have been occasional pathologies of Catholicism which were not addressed either by church or the state. This book proposes that Catholics must be ready whenever necessary to combat the prevailing secularist culture – to realise the greatness of their calling and seek to rise to that level in the provision of education.

Schools need to work at seeking internal coherence as well as pursuing external support from a believing Catholic community. The popularity and success of Catholic schools in non-Christian societies have shown that it is possible for non-Christian parents to have a real appreciation of the high standards of Catholic education and to support schools in their mission. The next section turns to a step-by-step analysis of the standards a Catholic school should aim for in seeking to live up to its mandate.

*Endnotes*

**Pope Benedict's informative address to Catholic educators in the US** – see address to Catholic Educators at Catholic University of America, 17 April 2008 on www.vatican.va.

**The truths of faith and of reason never contradict one another** – see First Vatican Council, *Dogmatic Constitution on the Catholic Faith "Dei Filius," IV: DS 3017*. Also see St. Augustine, *Contra Academicos, III, 20, 43*).

**'Catholic schools, which always strive to join…'** quote from Pope Francis – see his apostolic letter *The Joy of the Gospel pt 134*. '

**consultation process around the divestment of a Catholic primary school** – relates to proposed divestment of Scoil Naomh Mearnóg and Scoil An Duinninigh in north Dublin.

**Archbishop Eamon Martin quotation** – from an address '*The Catholic School and the New Evangelisation*' to Edmund Rice Trust Annual Foundation in Belfast on 20 February 2014

# SECTION 4
# Catholic education – making it happen

More than ever, it's crucial for schools to be able to explain what exactly happens within their four walls in the context of their characteristic spirit. Schools may not have 'competitor' schools at present but that is likely to change in the coming years as a greater plurality of school types is provided.

More importantly, school staff need to fully understand the characteristic spirit if they are to live it. An explained ethos can become a lived ethos, and actions speak louder than words. A school's academic team is its prime asset and, if properly empowered, they are uniquely placed to help spread the values the school strives for.

The next few chapters will look at how having a Catholic guiding spirit should impact on the approach to academics, character education, curriculum, prayer life (piety) and on the school as a professional environment. Included also is a brief overview of educational lacunae which undermine the effectiveness of Catholic schools in Ireland. Addressing these will undoubtedly improve the value of the product on offer.

The Catholic brand in education is an international top-class brand. Schools seeking to maintain that reputation do well to pay attention to all the key elements that make Catholic education so successful.

# Chapter 10
# Helping your school to be Catholic

> *Key Takeaways*
>
> *Because of the clashes between the dominant secular culture and Catholic culture, Catholic schools need to work harder to achieve their educational goals.*
>
> *Catholic education is possible in Ireland where schools have a clear vision, pursue it and are supported in that task. Misuse of the Catholic brand undermines its value.*
>
> *Catholic tradition acknowledges parents as primary educators and seeks to instil a welcoming family tone in schools.*
>
> *Catholic schools seek the all-round education of the young person and can achieve more when working with parish communities.*
>
> *Catholic schools are inclusive and recognise religious liberty, without denying their understanding of the truth.*

**Education takes place within a culture**

All of society progresses through time. Ideas, approaches, experiences leave their mark and form the culture of that society. Irish society has a culture with visible and invisible threads to the past, and many things seek to alter that culture as it passes through time.

The Christian faith came into the world with the claim – among others – that Jesus is truth in person and thereby is best placed to teach humankind about itself – to teach men and women what it means to be fully human. The faith is multilayered, with roots going back to Abraham.

This Christian faith also passes through time and exists as a culture. It weaves its way into other cultures over the generations giving meaning to, or drawing meaning from, things, while not displacing that which is true in the cultures into which the faith is woven. So you can be Catholic and Irish or Catholic and Vietnamese or whatever. The imprints that Catholic-Christianity leaves on the cultures which embrace it are deeply enriching.

However, the Catholic-Christian culture hasn't always sat easily with all other cultures, as it doesn't do so today in the increasingly secularized west. Paraphrasing St Paul, to some Christianity is seen as scandalous, while to others it is seen as foolishness.

This Catholic-Christian culture cannot hide itself away or avoid the clashes that arise because at its heart lies a command to go and teach all nations, to share the truth about God, about humanity and about eternal life.

All education takes place within a culture. It is a somewhat easier task to educate when there is some uniformity or conformity across the cultural influences experienced by a person, as was the case in Ireland in previous generations. Where a clash of cultures arises, education becomes a much more demanding engagement.

Such a direct clash of cultures now exists within Ireland. There is a clear dominant secularist culture which controls most of the levers of influence and power, and which is strongly promoted by a powerful media, a media which maintains a reasonable level of trust – albeit much reduced – within Irish society. And there is a Catholic culture which is gradually awakening to the fact that it has been sidelined.

Given this clash, if Catholic schools wish to educate Irish society in goodness and holiness they will have to work very hard at it, and likely have to do so with much more robustness. Should they manage to do the job successfully then they can help to reinvigorate a floundering Western culture.

The maintenance of the Christian faith is a generational challenge, and each generation has to educate the next one coming along. Schools have an important role to play in supporting families in this work.

**Can real Catholic education take place in Ireland today?**

Can schools still educate in the Catholic faith? Can they play their part in transmitting faith to the next generation? This is not quite as impossible a task as is sometimes made out.

For a start, Ireland has a Constitution which guarantees freedom of expression, freedom of assembly, freedom of association, freedom of conscience, freedom to practice religion and it is one in which the State also guarantees not to discriminate on the grounds of religion.

Secondly, the Irish school system empowers patron bodies in legislation and *requires* that schools have a specific 'characteristic spirit' or 'ethos'. So even though the new Junior Cycle Wellbeing syllabus embraces a secularised worldview, it still does (admittedly rather gently) defer to a school's culture and ethos. Although the overall Framework for the new Junior Cycle at second level is more in keeping with a relativistic and pragmatic view of education, it can be understood and followed in ways which are compatible with Catholic education. Thus, while there may be secularist pressures on schools (especially now on primary schools due to a proposed new draft curriculum on the horizon) there are still good reasons to believe that schools anchoring in their specific Catholic character have the capacity to counteract the excesses of a secularist culture.

Then, leaving aside for the present the specific challenges of the proposed new primary curriculum, can an Irish primary or secondary school educate within the Catholic tradition?

From a legal perspective the answer is clearly yes. This does require the patron body to have a strong vision as to what the school is about so that the school leaders can thread their way through the secularist minefield that is currently being laid down. Consequently, clarity about what it means to be Catholic, a good leadership team which understands and believes in the vision, and sufficient teachers and parents who will promote that vision are all needed. That need not be a large number of persons – as there are also many who will readily follow the leadership provided – but a core group must be committed to the task. And it is important for students and for Irish society that secondary schools educate clearly within the Catholic tradition since the third-level system that students face is strongly pragmatic and relativistic.

## Schools are central to people's lives

Education and the school where one is educated receive far more attention nowadays than ever before. While the unnecessary high visibility given to school league tables and to the Leaving Certificate are included in that, there is a much wider phenomenon happening as well.

One often sees a person described as a thirteen-year-old 'schoolboy', as if he might be something other than that. Or when something happens with a young person's Instagram account, or there is a bullying incident, or a suicide, or an accident, the media often frame the issue in the context of the person's school, or seek the school's response, as if it is somehow a key factor. This is seldom the case with an adult's place of employment. The fact is that with ever-increasing demands on parents' time, and with the content of learning dramatically evolving even within one generation, the school has become the place where most learning is expected to take place, where all the influences are expected to happen, and the school is viewed as if it were the guardian of the child.

## The Catholic brand

In speaking about schools, the term 'characteristic spirit', rather than 'ethos' is used in legal documents (as for example in the 1998 Education Act). That Act requires that a school use its available resources 'to promote the moral, spiritual, social and personal development of students and provide health education for them, in consultation with their parents, having regard to the characteristic spirit of the school.'

This phrase acknowledges that education is a holistic undertaking and that schools *should* undertake this task in line with the school's own defined characteristic spirit.

Most schools use their website to explain their characteristic spirit. Often such explanations highlight the specific holistic approach of Catholic education; the role of parent as primary educator; the links between families, the school and the parish community; and the call to Christian discipleship in addressing the burdens of life for each other.

Having clearly outlined what the Catholic brand means for the school, the challenge for any school community is to then live up to those demands. A school cannot allow that this be a brand of convenience or a slick marketing ploy to gain an advantage. To do so would be to contradict the Gospel and be disloyal to the brand as well as undermining the value of the brand for other schools and for other Catholic undertakings.

**Alternative brands**

At a time when faith-based institutions are being given the cold shoulder in the now-secular public square it is not easy to be counter-cultural. Yet a school needs to be proud of the brand, at a minimum never ashamed, aware of its educational strength, and ready to defend its inclusiveness and general value as compared to that of alternative non-Catholic brands.

As previously mentioned, as part of the divesting process of a particular primary school, a recent consultation with families chose to highlight how divestment would impact on Christian cultural celebrations and the conducting of faith formation outside of school hours. While these are clear tangible aspects of the Catholic educational brand they are but the tip of the iceberg. Catholic schools have a duty to understand more deeply their Catholic role in serving their community and wider society, and to share that understanding fully with parents.

As in any battle of brands, the value of the brand needs to highlighted and promoted, if it is to be continually embraced by our restless society. A brand is easily sullied, especially if very disappointing past performances of related Catholic brands are presented in an incomplete light. It can be very challenging for any institution to deal with a past for which it is not directly responsible especially when only its worst elements are highlighted. As mentioned earlier, media write-ups on the state-commissioned Mother and Baby Homes Report in early 2021, not happy that sufficient blame was attributed to the Catholic Church, embarked on selective anti-Catholic diatribes. The failings and wrongdoing of others reflects only on the culprits themselves and should not be allowed to tarnish the good and great deeds of many involved in providing true Catholic education. Unforgiving, selective media-reporting should serve as a positive spur to Catholic educators – knowing that the faith can often be a sign of contradiction – to live out their roles better, no matter how difficult that may at times appear.

## Parents as primary educators

In the Catholic tradition parents are acknowledged as the primary educators, with schools seeking to support them in that task. Schools operating with a Catholic ethos see education as an all-encompassing responsibility seeking to help students acquire the age-appropriate intellectual, spiritual, emotional, cultural and social maturity.

Parents look to schools for leadership to assist them in their overall education task. Schools do not undertake to mirror all of a parent's priorities, but rather to teach the child in line with a specific ethos, respecting personal freedom. Thus, in every school, irrespective of declared ethos, there will not always be full agreement with all families on aspects of the school's education or curriculum. It is important that there are open and clear channels of communication between the school and the home. A parent who feels welcome in a school is a parent who can come to trust the school. Unfortunately, budgetary constrictions on staffing in schools can hamper such communication, so home-school liaison teachers and active parent groups play an important role in making schools very accessible to all parents so that they can better understand the aims and objectives of the curriculum.

A school that is strong on its Catholic ethos will seek to see itself as an extension of the home, helping students appreciate the importance of family life and so preparing them for their future family responsibilities. The ideal parent-child interaction is the one to be modelled in the school between all staff members and all students, and thus one which the school will promote to its parents. And just as a parent may love each child equally but differently, this familial tone should shape all adult-child relationships within the school, including even the administration of school discipline.

It is always a great boon to any community when a school is constantly seeking ways to encourage school, parents and families to get to know each other better.

A school achieving this family spirit is a school which can easily welcome students and families from diverse backgrounds. Families by their nature are diverse institutions and are places where individuals learn to live with each other, ensuring that what they have in common can, over time, supersede individual differences. The school presents family living in the best manner that it can, and this seldom requires judgement on individual circumstances. In a family, difference can be respected without having to deny any underlying realities. This is a model which many Catholic-ethos schools have successfully implemented over centuries, realising as well, of course, that all tolerance has limits.

**Holistic education**

In a Catholic school the academic, spiritual, personal, social, and moral development of the child or young person are all of a piece. The school seeks to look after all dimensions of the young person, starting from the basis that each person is willed by God and has a meaning and purpose in life.

Financial or enrolment pressures leading to increasing school sizes can become an unacceptable excuse for accepting greater anonymity with regard to students in a school's care. The Catholic approach requires that the school seek to manage scale in such a way that each person understands their value as a person and that they are a known person within the school community.

Pressures to increase school numbers at second-level so as to improve the range of subjects available may sometimes derive from a misplaced appreciation of what is important in the school community. If personal anonymity becomes the result then the gain is a mirage. (There is a real danger that such pressures might become the norm if the reform of the Leaving Certificate is allowed to evolve around fulfilling 'needs' for a wider range of subjects.)

A young person's self-understanding is well supported by a school which fully explains its own specific purposes to the student, and which appreciates and understands the student in all his or her originality. Regular school assemblies are a reliable means whereby the school can present its values, hopes, expectations and aspirations to its students so as to win their allegiance.

**School and parish working together**

For many Catholic schools their structure ties them into a parish community. Where this is done well it relieves a lot of pressure on the school, allowing the parish 'village' to help educate the child. Outreach programmes which can have a profound lifelong impact on participants can often be easier to manage where there is a good parish structure. Youth branches of Catholic groups such as St Vincent de Paul Society, pilgrimage support groups for helpers on trips to Lourdes, educational visits to orphanages to countries such as Romania or Uganda may all be realistic possibilities where the school works closely with parishes and the responsibility is not all left with the school. Parish structures may become in time the main means of catechising for some young people, and will likely play an increasing role in the preparation for sacraments in the years ahead. In that regard there may be a role for someone to represent the school management on a local parish council. It is not that the school should do the job of the parish, but rather as an educational institution it should be able to draw on parish goodwill to help it live up to its demanding Catholic mandate. Any reforms of parish structures or services envisaged in the coming years should give consideration to the pivotal role a school can play in parish life.

**Being Catholic is to be inclusive**

A Catholic school seeks to foster a respect for all, regardless of personal talents, creed or social standing, helping everyone to be valued as persons. Most Irish Catholic schools have students from diverse cultural and religious backgrounds and nationalities, citizens of the world, living in a globalised culture, who need to be helped to be true to their faith by knowing it, so that they can re-present it to others. The ideal of the Catholic life can be presented in a school where an atmosphere of respect, trust and openness prevail. Catholicism, unlike secularism, does not impose since it fully recognises religious liberty, without denying its own understanding of where truth lies. Education in freedom is an important part of education for the world, and the Catholic school needs to propose an ideal for all young people to consider, help them see how to live out that ideal as well as helping them respect others who don't share that ideal in full or at all.

*Endnotes*

**2021 Mother and Baby Homes Report** – see *Final Report of the Commission of Investigation into Mother and Baby Homes,* published by Department of Children, January 2021.

**Catholicism, unlike secularism, does not impose** – see for example Pope Benedict XVI *Homily,* 14 May, 2010: 'We impose nothing, yet we propose ceaselessly, as Peter recommends in one of his Letters: "In your hearts reverence Christ as Lord. Always be prepared to make a defence to anyone who calls you to account for the hope that is in you" (I Peter 3:15). And everyone, in the end, asks this of us, even those who seem not to. From personal and communal experience we know well that it is Jesus whom everyone awaits.'

# Chapter 11
# Are Catholic schools doing anything wrong?

> *Key Takeaways*
>
> *The dominance of the secular culture should be a spur to Catholic schools to have a stronger sense of ethos.*
>
> *Catholic schools have made past mistakes and need to address their weaknesses. These include:*
> - *seeing Catholic education primarily in terms of promoting religious duties;*
> - *not prioritising character education;*
> - *weak links being made between Catholicism and daily living;*
> - *poorly explaining the Christian idea of freedom;*
> - *allowing compassion to be reduced to feelings;*
> - *misunderstanding charity;*
> - *poorly explaining moral decision-making;*
> - *imparting a weak understanding of conscience;*
> - *not alerting people adequately to the failings of the secular culture.*
>
> *More ambition with regard to charity and to explaining the adventure of Christian living is encouraged.*
>
> *Additionally, a greater openness to new educational methods might benefit all schools.*

**Are all Catholic schools really Catholic?**

Around 90% of schools at primary level and over 60% at secondary level claim a Catholic ethos, with some going to great lengths on websites and school prospectuses to affirm their catholicism. Yet some parents also complain that their local school is not *really* Catholic.

Could that be true? How can one evaluate whether Catholic schools are really Catholic, or whether their ethos is actually making a positive difference to their students and thus in society at large?

Certainly there are pointers that indicate strong marks of catholicity. International comparators on academic performance do show a strong commitment to academic excellence in Ireland. The obvious and demanding voluntary commitment required to run and maintain schools indicates a good community spirit and evidence of a strong Christian sense of duty. The country as a whole is a stable peace-loving society – which indicates something very positive about its underlying prevailing religious spirit. Irish society can display outrage at injustice, an indicator of a good level of religious sentiment and this is no bad thing, although, on the other hand, our society is slow in responding to obvious practical injustices in its midst: to use a biblical analogy, this may indicate that we are quick at rending our garments but slower in rending our hearts.

Other indicators could suggest failings in Catholic education. Church attendance is in steady decline especially among the younger generation. Young people tend to be more poorly catechised than their parents. One survey found Irish youth (aged 14 to 25 years) to be lost and curious, with a muddled understanding of core Christian beliefs, struggling to anchor their sense of morality. There are far fewer vocations to the priesthood and the religious life than are required to sustain the faith in the country, and there is a growing dependence in Irish parishes on priests from abroad. Family life as judged by marriage breakdown rates is not as secure as it once was. We tolerate high levels of homelessness. We blame moral ills in our society on poverty, yet such ills were not as prevalent when we were poorer. We have no true way to measure how many Irish people see holiness as an adventure, but may presume from the dearth of public witness that, however many these may be, it is primarily viewed as a private task.

Some school trustees, boards of management and teachers, conscious of their own school's lack of allegiance to Catholicism will argue that they would like to have a stronger sense of ethos but that the reality of the classroom dictates how things turn out – in short, the Catholic culture is becoming submerged by the wider secularism that prevails, and they are experiencing or presuming a degree of helplessness in response.

Rather than lessen a school's commitment to its Catholicity, this classroom reality should be a spur to make Catholicism more palatable for students. The sense of a loss of purpose evident in society can only be addressed by giving young people strong reference points, and a Catholic education in freedom makes it easier for young people to find their way in the world.

There are also many other schools – proud of their origins and intent on doing things well – who feel that they are not quite hitting the mark, despite a real effort to provide a genuine Catholic culture within their school and among the wider community.

All that said, a common denominator across very many Catholic schools is that they would wish to be more in tune with their ethos. In that context, it is good to identify the sort of things that may be going wrong by comparing the present reality with the ideal of a Catholic education. Where are schools falling down in the delivery of a Catholic ethos? How can they be helped to be more ambitious in their intent? Acknowledging mistakes can be a first step on the road to improving the quality of Catholic education provided by schools. What follows is an identification of twelve broad areas where Catholic schools can improve, or indeed areas where they might need further supports from Catholic education authorities.

**Twelve areas with scope for improvement**

**1. The person of Jesus Christ should precede the piety**
There has been a historical tendency in Irish Catholicism to associate the Catholic faith primarily with piety (see Chapter 15 for a full explanation of this term) – especially public prayer – to the detriment of the wider influences of faith. Many may only appreciate their Catholicism in liturgical and personal piety terms. Young people certainly do need to learn the importance of prayer and of liturgy, but it needs to be anchored in ordinary life. Big liturgical occasions are important, but should lead to or be directed towards helping young people appreciate the graces received through the more ordinary liturgical occasions. Liturgical occasions focussed on the parish and the family are more likely to be sustained than once-off events proposed by the school.

First and foremost, schools need to present to young people that Christianity is about following in the footsteps of a person, Jesus Christ. In the words of Pope Benedict,

> Being a Christian is not the result of an ethical choice or a lofty idea but the encounter with an event, a person, which gives life a new horizon and a decisive direction.

It is in the context then of getting to know the person of Jesus Christ and desiring to follow him that piety and liturgy have their parts to play. So, education needs to first point out Christ the person (true God and true man), thus providing them a basis for worship (including liturgy), prayer and also morality.

And a sixteen-year-old's understanding of the person of Christ must have moved way beyond what that person understood six years earlier! In primary school basic knowledge of the faith must be imparted – mysteries and all – whereas enquiring secondary-school students should rightly delve into the background of these mysteries and of how the Church has managed to unpack them over the centuries. A syllabus must seek to present Christ as true God and true man if one is to understand what it is to pray.

## 2. Laying the building blocks of character

The Catholic commitment to a holistic education requires the provision of a systematic education in virtues or good habits. Counter-cultural challenges can overwhelm people from an early age, so the school and family need to work at building up a young person's inner strength though living virtues, building blocks that ultimately assist the person in the search for truth.

Education is not simply a question of exhorting young people to be good: they have to be helped to be so. Education in courage, self-denial, generosity, humility and cheerfulness is as least as important as education in any civic virtue. This is the stuff of character education – and it should underpin all areas within the school as well as forming a strong bridge between the educational efforts of the Catholic school and the home.

A person who appreciates virtue is someone with an improved capacity to learn and to put the demands of Christian living into effect. The great Catholic educator St Thomas Aquinas saw virtue ethics come into play in all aspects of teaching and learning – for him the virtues of the teacher were modelled on Christ the great teacher, as were the virtues of learning on the young Christ who 'grew in wisdom and stature' (*St Luke's Gospel, 2:52*).

Formation in virtue is not some clandestine undertaking. The laying of the building blocks of character requires a whole school programme and commitment.

### 3. Christian ordinariness

Catholic education should include an understanding that an aspect of being Catholic is to do all one's ordinary things, especially one's academic work, as best one can, following in the footsteps of the master who 'has done all things well' (*St Mark's Gospel, 7:37*). Young people should be educated to realise that their efforts to do their work well, to be more sociable with their fellow students and to contribute to their family life are as much part of being Catholic as are their efforts to do the right thing (that is, morality). Catholic schools should consistently remind their students of the greatness – temporal and eternal – that lies in the ordinary things of life, and their own greatness – as children of God – in that context.

A school's curriculum must not allow an understanding of the Catholic worldview to be reduced to major political issues. Certainly, abortion and corruption and global warming and free speech all have significant moral dimensions where the right answers are important. Yet, unless a young person imbibes and lives his or her Catholic faith in ordinary things such as one's academic studies and relationships then he or she is less likely to understand or fully take to heart a Catholic vision.

### 4. Educating for freedom

In recent years the portrayal of the clash between the Catholic and secular worldviews in areas of sexual morality has limited many adult Catholics' appreciation of the scope of their faith. Few young people fully appreciate the Catholic grasp of truth. Understanding the battle between the 'civilisation of life' and the 'culture of death' – to use the terminology of Pope St John Paul II – continues to be very important, but there are also other fundamental issues on which Catholicism has much to teach the world.

In the coming decades, as secularism moves to deny that there is any normative behaviour whatever – or any form of 'right' behaviour – and to deny basic democratic freedoms, it may well become easier for people to understand how much Catholicism is actually on the side of human freedom. Young people need help to appreciate that it is Christianity – with its commitment to natural law – that has made democracy and democratic freedoms possible (such as freedoms of belief, of expression and of assembly). By explaining the links between Catholicism, reason, nature and freedom not only will democracy be supported but young people will be helped to better understand how Catholicism has also got it right in the areas of human sexuality.

## 5. Misplaced compassion

Most schools emphasise the importance of loving one's neighbour, and work hard to create a good classroom spirit while encouraging and providing opportunities of service, especially in Transition Year. Yet young Irish adults have shown that they misunderstand basic principles of Christian compassion, despite an almost universal emphasis on charity in Catholic schools. So has anything gone wrong?

Schools cannot allow that the living of charity be reduced in a young person's mind to feeling good about what they do for others. Putting money in a Trócaire box should never be about appeasing one's feelings.

Students need help to understand that any immediate reward that comes from serving others should be directed towards growing in humility, gratitude and a desire to serve God and our fellow human beings more, and not to self-congratulation or feeling good about oneself. Such feelings leave a person's capacity for compassion open to manipulation. A false compassion for abusers contributed to the disastrous, recently-acquired reputation of the Catholic Church. One should recall that there were many who would have preferred Jesus to come down from the Cross, whilst very few showed the genuine compassion – the suffering with – of his Mother Mary and the young St John, who understood that God's will rules over man's.

Allowing compassion to be reduced to feelings creates a world where over-needy individuals or unscrupulous advertisers enjoy the advantage, enabling them to explain away almost any wrong or to make evil sound as if it were good. This is even truer in our new empathy-driven world divided into victims and oppressors where any response of a 'victim', despite its immorality, is seemingly justified.

The Christian way is one of compassion associated with reason, so education in moral reasoning cannot be neglected. The displacement of reason by feelings in the making of moral decisions is the cause of much moral turmoil for young people. So often one hears it said that 'I felt it was the right thing to do' meaning exactly that – the decision was based on feelings, and not a decision of the whole person, guided by reason. Teenagers are more apt to indulge their emotions, so it is vital that they hear much more about the role of reason. Schools need to revisit how they educate in managing emotions and in moral decision-making.

**6. Understanding charity**
Too often in our society, people reduce charity to issues of justice or see it in terms of equality. There will always be injustices to be combatted, but charity has a deeper personal remit. Perhaps the best educational way to understand Christian charity is to consider the parable of the Good Samaritan. He saw the needs of the Jew who had been robbed, and he provided for these by doing what he could and by also involving the innkeeper in the plan. The fact that Jews looked down on Samaritans did not deter him – he had crossed paths with a fellow human being in need and he responded accordingly. For the Good Samaritan equality was not a consideration nor a motivation, but restoration was.

It is noble to seek to create equality of opportunity for all human beings, starting with those in our own circle of influence. It is noble to help others. It is also Christian to seek justice for others. But charity for the Christian is a deeper response – it is, paraphrasing St Teresa of Calcutta, to see the face of Jesus in others and to be motivated to respond to that person's need. Christians don't perform charity simply because they perceive a lack of justice in a given situation: they do so because they see another human being in need. Without this full understanding, Catholics are open to imbibe the misplaced woke culture of social justice, just as misunderstanding charity in the previous century made it difficult for some Catholics to resist the false egalitarian lure of communism.

**7. The charitable vision of the school**
In this book, various exhortations are made to living charity. The vision of a Catholic school in that regard can be boundless. Cardinal Ratzinger (later Pope Benedict XVI) in a Holy Week reflection on Christ's washing the feet of his disciples, a task allocated to slaves, reminded Christians of the standard Christ set for his followers: 'If I then, your Lord and teacher have washed your feet, you also ought to wash one another's feet.' (St Johns Gospel 13:14). For Cardinal Ratzinger,

John expresses a very important truth: love in the abstract will never have any force in the world if it does not sink its roots in the actual community built in fraternal love.

Rather than having a vision bounded or limited by the realities and challenges in the local community, a school can seek to transcend these and, over time, bring the whole community along. Young people wish to have their idealism stimulated and welcome any encouraging leadership. A school united around its ethos is well placed to do that. Thus Catholic schools, like the great monasteries of old, can have the ambition of seeking to be genuine fraternal communities which have a perennial influence on their locality.

### 8. The adventure of Christian living
According to Finola Kennedy, as far back as the middle of the last century, Frank Duff, the founder of the Legion of Mary, was complaining that in Ireland 'Catholicism was not been practised sufficiently as a social religion, concerned with duty in every shape and form towards one's fellow people, individually and corporately.' Subsequently, the Second Vatican Council reminded all Catholics that each person is 'a witness and a living instrument of the Church itself.'

Greater emphasis needs to be given in Catholic school curricula and by educators to this call to apostolic mission in our world. The prevailing secular ideas of choice and individualism combined with a culture of non-judgementalism are swamping any sense that Catholics are called to help not only themselves but also their families, friends and colleagues along the path to heaven. Schools are relatively good at highlighting corporal works of mercy – at least on the social level. By comparison, they are relatively weak in promoting the spiritual works of mercy to be lived on an individual level.

The adventure of Christian living does not centre on sporting success and prowess, important as these may be as part of personal development in schools. No, the adventure is about Catholics being empowered through their personal relationship with God to share that treasure with many others and to live within the horizon of eternal life. This leads to Catholics proposing and re-proposing the values of Christian living to their friends while being a support, countering weakness and distractions along the path. In turn, this requires that Catholics be clear on what Christian living is, and how it is achievable.

For example, countering the culture of alcohol abuse, so prevalent and destructive within Irish society, is a clear area for greater Christian witness. Better education or greater commitment to the virtue of chastity would lead to fewer persons being exploited by the culture or by degrading commercial forces. In short, young Catholics need to understand how to help their friends to live out their faith in the ordinary everyday challenges they face. The lost years regretted afterwards by so many young people would be fewer it Catholics in their school years were helped to understand and live their apostolic mission, firstly among their friends and colleagues.

**9. It is holistic for a reason**
All-round education of the person is the Catholic ideal, and it is so for a reason. Apart from seeking to emulate the 'perfect man' dimension of Jesus Christ – 'true God and true man' – the Catholic tradition understands that a fully human action is an action of the whole person and not solely a rational response or an emotional response to any human reality.

Moral decision-making is not a question of feelings but rather of understanding objective right and wrong. Feelings are indicators: yes, and these are sometimes reliable, but equally sometimes they are not. When a person decides to carry out an act, ideally it is the whole person who is acting and it should be the whole person involved in the decision-making: memory, reason and will. The memory situates the person in history, recalls the nature of the human person as creature, and explains the lessons of the past. Our emotions remind us of who we are and anchor us in our neighbourliness. Our reason allows us to reflect on the reality of our existence, the nature of God, the common good and the competing interests before us. Reason becomes more specific when facing a choice, and, guided by God's voice within us, the natural law, our conscience directs us towards the right choice. Our will then decides and guides our rationally and emotionally motivated action.

Young people need to be well informed in the process of moral reasoning if they are to move beyond emotional responses which the wider culture seeks to intensify for them. Feelings are but one part of who we are.

**10. Resisting the lure of Utopia**
In the past, young poorly-formed Christians were easy prey for communism, with its stress on equality, seeing it as a possible way to address real injustices

within society. It took the revelation of the real-world experience of Soviet communism in the 1960s to remove the scales from many people's eyes. Nowadays, similarly poorly-educated Catholics fall prey to the utopian world of social justice. Being 'woke' implies a belief that we are surrounded by systemic injustices and leads ultimately to a solution of exclusion and violence, and non-engagement with others, even the demonisation of individuals and whole categories of people, thus excluding all pathways to reconciliation. Moving the compassionate hearts of students to address injustice in the world is a sorely deficient education unless they are also given the intellectual tools to ensure that their reason and emotions work together and in harmony.

Compassionate-minded young people can also find that their moral decision-making can easily be overridden by emotional over-engagement simply because they are inadequately instructed in objective reason, and the role of subjective reason – conscience. They understand conscience to be an extension of their feelings, and not what it is – that is, when truly informed – the voice of God within.

Utopias are normally constructed around kernels of truth, and thus under-educated, well-meaning Catholics, big on justice and low in their understanding of the human person, can swallow utopias built on the promised delivery of social justice. Catholic education, working through the wide scope provided in school curricula, must lead young people to seek the fundamental truth of things so that they do not become victims to partial truths.

**11. Knowing where you swim**
Perhaps the biggest failing of Irish Catholic education is its inability to identify for young people the fatal weaknesses in the prevailing culture. An underlining theme of this book is to portray how the Catholic-Christian worldview is so fundamentally different from that of our wider secular society. These differences have increased enormously over the past generation as the mainstream culture has moved away from its Christian roots, but, by and large, Catholic schools have not learned how to educate counter-culturally. More often than not they have lacked the confidence of their convictions and/or are unable to communicate those convictions in a secular culture which constantly misuses Christian terminology to achieve its ends.

Some may argue that our secular society may have wealth of its own to impart.

Indeed, as with all cultures, there may be some commonalities. For example, both cultures appreciate a role for (scientific) reason as a guide in decision-making, but differ on its degree of importance.

Yet the world-wide, two-centuries-old Catholic Church's teaching authority's reluctance to cede ground to secularism should be a source of strength to Catholic schools in realising that at this moment in the world's history they are called to be counter-cultural.

Many of the possible deficiencies in the Catholic education already identified above relate more to the content of learning and less to pedagogy. As time passes, Christian pedagogy may also come under threat, as the role of teacher as an educator in truth comes under the 'woke' spotlight – a topic discussed in more detail in chapter 21.

Undoubtedly, there is a need for coherent character-development programmes and structured religious education syllabi. Commitment is also required to communicate Catholic culture – not just in religion class but throughout the school curriculum. Teachers of English, History, Science, Politics, Music or Art all have ample and professionally-purposeful opportunities to deal with questions such as objective truth, morality, conscience and the content of charity through their curricula. But they must have a living awareness of what needs to be done – as well as the practical wherewithal – if they are to do this. There are insufficient supports currently available within Irish schools to help teachers sustain such a Catholic culture or to help schools wishing to put a Catholic ethos fully into practice. With supportive resources (which will often need to be funded and provided by Catholic sources or Catholic colleges of education) and good internal dialogue on ethos, many schools can be hopeful of making great strides in delivering a strong antidote to secularism.

## 12. Being ready to try new things

An innate conservatism dominates an Irish school system which has shown very few attempts to try out other education models. The enormous developments in online learning have had little impact on how lessons are imparted in schools. While this lack of experimentation may be due mainly to standardised expectations set by the Leaving Certificate exam system, or by teacher unions or centralised education models promoted by Department of Education, Catholic educators could do much better in pushing out the boat, with a view to improving the quality of education provided to young people. It is not the focus of this book to question the overall effectiveness of the Irish education system. Yet Catholic educators would be advised not to feel constrained by the conservatism that persists and be ready to show leadership in promoting new models of schooling should these be more appropriate for students and for our present age.

In an informative newspaper interview, the head of education for the OECD, Dr Andreas Schleicher said that positive features of the Irish education system included the strong value placed on education by society, a reasonably good track record in providing educational opportunities to less well-off students, and good literacy standards when compared globally. But at the same time he pointed out that 'just 15% of Irish 15-year-olds can distinguish fact from opinion in a reliable way. So, you know, what value is literacy, if you can't navigate ambiguity? If we can't manage complexity?'

In the same interview, Dr Schleicher highlighted that despite our preoccupation with class size there was no correlation between this and tuition outcomes, with some high-performing countries having much bigger class sizes. For him, the issue was how resources were used in terms of teacher collaboration and individual students' needs – a call for educationalists to be more ready to think outside the box in meeting students' needs, and an area where more innovation may be called for.

Dr Schleicher also indicated that key challenges for Irish schools included getting students to think for themselves, and to develop a strong sense of right and wrong. Despite superficial arguments to the contrary, Catholic schools provide an ideal environment for education because the Catholic faith is rationally grounded and a champion of rationality. Dr Schleicher's observations also reinforce a number of the points made above about education in morality, and how well placed a comprehensive Catholic education is to serve the students of tomorrow.

We have a second-level school system where young adults follow much the same procedures, rules and class schedules as children, and often are treated in much the same way. We have teachers who have apprehensions about appraising students they may have taught for many years. We have schools now dominated by subject departments, as if the subjects were mainly what education was about. We continue to have a senior-school system in the straightjacket shaped by the final school examination. We have no general social credits system, no recognition within the school system of the community involvement of young people nor is any real value placed on education that takes place beyond the school doors. Much is as it was before the advent of television, not to mention the advances of new technologies and the internet.

The zoom experiences of 2020 and 2021 have shown that schools can operate differently. There are excellent resources now available online which, when used innovatively, can allow teachers to use their time differently. While all experimentation in teaching and learning may be subject to the approval of other partners in education, Catholic educators, with a view towards educating young people for life, should seek to be at the forefront of innovation within schools.

**A name for all this**
Catholic schools and teachers would do well to always consider the measure of their work. And ask: to what standard have the minds and hearts of their students been filled?

Pope Benedict XVI has given this standard a name: 'intellectual charity'. In an address to US Catholic educators in 2008, he spoke of the need to cultivate this when he said:

> (I)ntellectual charity calls the educator to recognize that the profound responsibility to lead the young to truth is nothing less than an act of love. Indeed, the dignity of education lies in fostering the true perfection and happiness of those to be educated. In practice 'intellectual charity' upholds the essential unity of knowledge against the fragmentation which ensues when reason is detached from the pursuit of truth... Once their passion for the fullness and unity of truth has been awakened, young people will surely relish the discovery that the question of what they can know opens up the vast adventure of what they ought to do. Here they will experience 'in what' and 'in whom' it is possible to hope, and be inspired to contribute to society in a way that engenders hope in others.

***Endnotes***

**One survey found Irish youth (aged 14 to 25 years) to be lost and curious** See *Finding Faith in Ireland – the Shifting Spiritual Landscape of Teens and Young Adults in the Republic of Ireland* (2017) on www.barna.com

**'Being a Christian is not the result of an ethical choice or a lofty idea'** – see Introduction to *Deus Caritas Est (On Christian Love)* by Pope Benedict (2005)

**Cardinal Ratzinger in a Holy Week reflection** – See *Journey to Easter* by Pope Benedict XVI (Crossroad Publishing, 2005)

**According to Finola Kennedy** – See *Frank Duff – a life story* by Finola Kennedy (Burns and Oates)

**Subsequently the Second Vatican Council said** – See Vatican Council II *Lumen Gentium* (n 33)

For **interview with Dr A Schleicher** – see Karl O'Brien *'Irish schools need to modernise "20th century" approach to learning'* in *The Irish Times,* 22 March 2021.

**Despite superficial arguments to the contrary** – critics complain that Catholicism does not teach Catholics to think for themselves, but to accept the teaching of the Church on blind faith. This is because many of these critics do not appreciate that Catholicism does actually depend on the interplay of faith and reason (reason being understood more broadly than the truncated reason of secularism). Catholicism is a champion of rationality - for example, the rationality of theism, the rationality of ethics/natural law, and the historicity of the Gospels and New Testament. Catholic education, and specifically Catholic religious education, is not only compatible with the development of critical reasoning but is even more so than alternative liberal models of religious education. For a deeper analysis of developing critical reasoning within religious education see '*Apology of the Reasonableness of Catholic Religious Education*' by Thomas Finegan, (*Louvain Studies* 43, 2020).

# Chapter 12
# Addressing academic standards

> *Key Takeaways*
>
> *The DES Quality Framework booklet is a very good guide to excellence in teaching and learning. Striving for academic excellence is part of the core mission of a Catholic school.*
>
> *Academic virtues such as a desire for excellence, ambition, perseverance and honesty should be promoted and pursued in a Catholic school.*
>
> *Students should be helped to see how different subjects fit together and point towards objective truth.*
>
> *Assessment methods must be inherently fair. All upcoming exam reform needs to avoid woke influences.*

**A quality framework**

In 2016, the Department of Education provided well-considered guidelines for the operation of schools in booklets entitled: '*Looking at Our School 2016: A Quality Framework for Primary/Post-Primary Schools*'. These frameworks which concerned the teaching, learning, leadership, and management within schools, were provided to support the efforts of teachers, school leaders, and the wider school system to strive for excellence in Irish schools.

Building on the high levels of confidence that Irish schools are well run, and conscious that maintaining and improving the quality of learning in schools is a constant challenge, these booklets provide valuable self-evaluation tools. Linking such self-evaluation with school inspections has raised the professional attention that has been given to these booklets since they first appeared.

The quality framework provides a clear picture of what good or very good practices in a school should look like. It allows schools to look at their own practices and to identify what they are doing well, and what aspects of the school's work could be further developed to improve students' learning experiences and outcomes. For a Catholic school these self-evaluation tools are great guides to helping the school live up to its ethos in the area of academic and professional excellence.

**Academic excellence**

Christ's 'doing all things well' (ref *St Mark's Gospel, 7:37*) is a call to excellence to which a Catholic school should respond. It extends to school policies, to the administrative and academic tasks in the school, to the quality of the school's surroundings, to the individual personal and learning needs of students, and to all interactions with its community. In a special way it applies to the search for academic excellence as this is the primary way for a school to set a young person's sights higher and for that person to live out their daily Christian calling. Part of the way Catholic schools can win allegiance of students to their faith is by showing how excellence in the work they do is part of their daily Christian calling. In this way being a Catholic Christian is no longer reduced in the students' minds to living moral rules – as it never should be – but is rather lived out in a daily response to following the person of Jesus Christ. Some success achieved along that path, for example through good quality work done for love of God, ultimately helps to make other moral challenges less spiritually daunting.

The good habit of doing one's academic work well also becomes a worthy stepping stone to the future, and encourages young people to make everything in this world, especially their future professional work, holy and pleasing in God's sight.

Some businesses seek to achieve a Q-mark or quality mark so as to enhance their position in the marketplace. Others do so because they simply wish to have an external measure of the high quality service they provide. Unfortunately for second-level schools over the past generation, because of the CAO points race, academic excellence has tended to be measured by Leaving Certificate outcomes. This high stakes once-off exam, with its own in-built and unacknowledged inequities has had a distorting impact on the quality of educational experience at senior cycle in our schools. Now with Covid-19 having exposed the examination's unnecessary rigidities and with a review of it being imminent following on the Junior Cycle reform, educationalists have the opportunity to re-evaluate what a quality education means and how it should be assessed going forward, without having to give primary consideration to the entry requirements of third-level colleges.

Efforts to achieve academic excellence within a Catholic school lead to a reputation for excellence emerging, which in turn encourages academically motivated students to choose the school, which further enhances the reputation for academic excellence. The means to make this happen, especially through teaching and learning, are well outlined in the Department of Education's Framework documents.

Striving for academic excellence is also a key motivator which will enhance character education in a school, a subject that will be addressed in the next chapter.

**Academic virtue**

An additional means of promoting and achieving academic excellence is to have a whole school approach in promoting growth in academic virtues.

The upcoming chapter on character education explains how virtues, or good habits, are liberating, freeing the person to go further or achieve more. The human virtues described there impact on all aspects of a person's life.

Some virtues have a greater bearing on the academic challenges: these we will call academic virtues. They include:

- A desire for excellence: i.e. seeking to produce good quality work. This in turn means working on those skills that will facilitate that e.g. researching things well, silent study, taking good notes, not rushing homework, planning answers, ready to go the extra mile, having a healthy competitive spirit, taking pride in the quality of work presented.

- Ambition – the 'proper amount' (as Aristotle says) and not more.

- Perseverance and persistence. This can lead to developing skills such as improved reading, handwriting, or analytical skills.

- Honesty. This will help a person to be fair in truly assessing one's own progress, and face up to challenges more easily, as well as avoiding plagiarism, dishonesty etc.

- Originality of thought. This is not necessarily a virtue which can be acquired in itself but one that can be facilitated through patience and open-mindedness in learning from others.

- Openness to helping others. Oftentimes a lot of learning can come about through understanding the mistakes of others.

There is an ever-increasing possible range of subjects that can be taught in schools, and even more so in universities, in response to increasingly diverse work opportunities. However, and insofar as there is a choice to be made, rather than giving primacy to more and more subjects in response to fragmentation, schools should centre on educating in key ideas and core skills.

There is also a unity of knowledge which a Catholic school should seek to impart. This is in opposition to a different sort of fragmentation – the one that occurs 'when reason is detached from the pursuit of truth.' If Catholic schools are to resist ideological interest-groups or the short-term pragmatic goals set by others, they need to understand the concept of unity of knowledge, and how subjects generally point towards the one objective truth. There is much to be learned from St John Henry Newman on the overall unity of knowledge and how different subjects fit together. We will briefly return to this in the upcoming chapter on curriculum.

Nor can Catholic schools give in to the demands of those who insist on giving equal value to practically everything. Our second-level education structures must be able to resist the pressure of fashionable or pragmatic arguments, and of powerful unanchored viewpoints which have no regard for history, tradition or academic learning. They should learn from the mistakes made in many humanities departments in third-level colleges – and now creeping into the sciences. In particular, the suspicion, scepticism and relativism generated by post-modernist thought should be kept at a long distance from primary and secondary schools, not allowing educational institutions become grounds for ideological experimentation.

Schools, in forming good habits of heart and mind, need to prepare students in those essential skills which colleges may now fail to teach – that is, open enquiry, constructive debate including disagreement, understanding the variety of viewpoints that exist, while teaching and promoting the search for objective truth.

## Assessment

Assessment plays a major role in all learning, and educational staff are well versed in all aspects of assessment of learning and assessment for learning. Helping young people themselves to understand their strengths and weaknesses can provide many with greater motivational power to improve.

There are a range of requirements on educators which a Catholic school should not overlook. Young people have a heightened sense of justice, so the methods of assessment should also be considered through the students' eyes. Students appreciate objectivity of teacher assessment as well as fairness in methodology and in results obtained. This requires appropriate time being given to a variety of assessment modes, as well as solid standardisation of marking across subjects and class groups. Undoubtedly, such co-ordination within a big school places additional pressure on middle management. With the new Junior Cycle programme teachers have become much more skilled in the task of assessment, and one should not underestimate the positive moral impact this can have on students' perception of fairness.

The proposed revision of the Leaving Certificate programme is a major challenge facing the education sector. The examination itself has clear weaknesses and strengths – for some a source of unparalleled mental stress, for others a vindication of a lot of very hard work. It is anticipated that any revision plan will give more consideration to continual assessment and project work over a two- or possibly three-year period. There will be many difficulties in getting this reform over the line. Many teachers do not want it to take place until the new Junior Cycle has had an external review. Others want the reforms already now built into the Junior Cycle to continue to roll on, otherwise all students will be disadvantaged. There is always the danger that a woke-culture approach to assessment per se – i.e. a drive to abolish assessment – might seek common cause with those conscious of the mental-health impacts of the high-stakes nature of the examination and all surrounding it. Viewed from a Christian perspective one would wish that the reshaped examination will continue to motivate students towards academic excellence – thus aiming to be an objective measure of achievement – while not disrupting good order in their personal lives.

*Endnotes*

**Academic Excellence:** Pope John Paul II's 1981 encyclical *On Human Work (Laborem Exercens)* gives a solid theological grounding for the importance of human work and it link to the dignity of man. Catholic social teaching more generally highlights how work is an integral part of human fulfilment for the individual and for society. The writings of St Josemaria Escriva (see *www.escrivaworks.org*) treat extensively of the sanctifying value of ordinary work and ordinary daily living.

**'when reason is detached from the pursuit of truth'** – see Meeting with Catholic Educators, 17 April 2008 – Pope Benedict XVI in Catholic University of America in Washington on www.vatican.va

**Woke culture approach to assessment** – see Chapter 21 for more details regarding the State of Oregon (USA)

# Chapter 13
# The building blocks of character

> *Key Takeaways*
>
> *A cultivated intellect is not character. Character education and training in virtue give young people tools of self-mastery, making it easier to do the good. It is an essential part of educating the whole person.*
>
> *Character education broadens the domain of one's personality traits.*
>
> *Character education must have charity at its heart – both in the educator and for the learner.*
>
> *One way students learn virtue is by seeing it modelled by educators.*

## What is character?

This idea of character is strongly associated with the pre-Christian philosopher Aristotle. It also has roots within the Hebrew tradition with its focus on holiness, honesty, justice, integrity, care for the poor, faithfulness to God, and on wisdom. These ideas have been carried forward into the present day primarily within the Judeo-Christian tradition.

The Book of Wisdom (Chapter 8:7) highlights the four main virtues of the Greek philosophers:

> And if anyone loves righteousness,
> her labours are virtues;
> for she teaches self-control and prudence,
> justice and courage:
> nothing in life is more profitable for men than these.

These cardinal virtues – prudence, justice, temperance and fortitude – help us to do the good thing. Together with the three theological virtues of faith hope and charity, these dispose us to 'become like God.'

Character has been defined as 'inner strength to do the right thing.'

A person of character is one who integrates the key traits or good habits that one would wish to have – habits such as sound judgement, sense of responsibility, courage, self-mastery, and generosity. Character education is then the process involved in helping young people acquire these key traits, virtues, or good habits.

As such, character education is the foundation on which personal development can be readily advanced with the goal of helping young people develop the good habits that will enable them to flourish intellectually, personally and socially.

The Irish educational system, although it espouses a holistic view of the person, has been slow to take on personal character development as a means of advancing overall educational objectives. Irish students can measure their History or Mathematics or Language abilities to the nearest one or two percent. They can well distinguish whether they have a B2 or B3 attainment in a particular academic subject at Leaving Certificate level. Many are able to quote passages at will from relatively obscure poetry or, in some cases, Sacred Scripture or even memorise complex Chemistry equations. Yet often they cannot even begin to give a reliable assessment or measure of how humble or courageous or industrious or charitable they are! A good student may even be able to recite the Ten Commandments by heart but have no real understanding of how formation in virtue can be of help in living up to the standards these set.

The great English educator St. John Henry Newman was very clear on the limitations of the liberal education he was proposing for his new university in Dublin in the 1850s. He distinguished between the enlargement of mind associated with a liberal education and a training in virtue (or what are called good habits) which he saw as a completely different challenge. He is worth quoting at length:

> To open the mind, to correct it, to refine it, to enable it to know, and to digest, master, rule and use its knowledge, to give it power over its own faculties, application, flexibility, method, critical exactness, sagacity, resource, address, eloquent expression is an object as intelligible as the cultivation of virtue, which at the same time is absolutely distinct from it.

## The building blocks of character

For Newman, 'liberal education makes not the Christian, nor the Catholic, but the gentleman'. He clearly stated that qualities such as a dispassionate mind and a cultivated intellect were not virtue. Many years later those wondering how well-educated German officers, who appreciated the great musicians of our age, could inflict such inhuman cruelty in death camps such as Auschwitz, have clearly not read Newman. Even today in Ireland, when we reflect on how we Irish could have got so many things in church and state so wrong, from our social institutions of the last century to our economic institutions of the present one, we would do well to consider how virtue is, or is not, imparted through our education system.

Yet good character traits are not equivalent to moral goodness, they just make it easier for the person to do the right thing. You can be very efficient because it suits you, but not because of any moral, social or charitable intent.

Why bother with such character education then? Why not leave it, as most education institutions currently do, to the informality of the life of the school? That is, let he or she pick it up as they go along.

Well, ultimately schools are seeking to prepare young persons for successful and happy lives. Freedom is an important part of that, and virtues or good habits are necessary for a student to rule passions and emotions so as to live freely. It is obvious that a person dominated by a passion such as anger is not free to do many things – in the same way as a person who doesn't learn to play the piano cannot later be 'free' to give a public piano recital. Formalising an education in virtue helps young people see the tools available to master themselves, helps provide the skills with which to use them, and alerts young minds to the existence of the good and the true.

**Personality is not character**

Psychology through the ages has tried to understand the human person. Two major approaches with which people are generally familiar are the ideas of temperament (moods) and personality. The understanding of temperaments of which there are four – sanguine, choleric, melancholic and phlegmatic – goes all the way back to 400 BC or thereabouts.

More recent psychology presents us instead with what are called personality traits or dispositions, which tend to be constant over time, and which can be partially cultural. Known as the Big Five traits – open to experience and intellect, conscientiousness, extraversion, agreeableness, and neuroticism – a person may be described as being a variable mix of all of these.

The person any child is, and will become, is shaped by many factors. The child has particular personality traits, some of which are deep-rooted, some of which are shaped by upbringing. It does help a parent, or indeed a teacher, to try to understand the personality of a child, not simply so as to apply a label, but to help the child come to understand themselves. The character bit comes next; it comes on top of who we are, so to speak. We are not determined by our personality and we can substantially broaden the domain of our personality traits through character education.

**Obstacles to learning**

When it comes to a child's learning, there are many intervening factors which may affect the quality of that learning. Some learning blockage or obstacle or disability – defined loosely as something which others usually have but which this child has not – can often be undiagnosed, and can have minor or major influences on a young person's learning. This may be due, for example, to some physical, chemical, or neurodevelopmental imbalance.

Some children have a great capacity to compensate for a disorder or blockage, thus masking the effect of any underlying disability, preventing it from coming to light until adolescence or perhaps never. These are not personality issues, but they can affect a person's behaviour, and they do impact on how one can understand behaviour. In that sense they have a part to play while discussing the topic of character education. There are also certain behaviours, which in the classroom lead to disruption, and which are given an appropriate label from that perspective, but which are possibly strengths in other environments. Someone described as 'having a talkative nature' springs immediately to mind!

Learning or behavioural difficulties may inhibit the development of some good character traits, or lessen the chance of these taking hold. This should not lead one to abandon efforts to inculcate character, but rather to be aware of the hurdles along the road. For example, it is well established that a learning disability like dyslexia can lead to underlying or unexpressed frustration in young people, leading to otherwise inexplicable aggressive outbursts. While it is important that the young person develop the virtue of calmness and composure, the bar may initially need to be set lower due to the disability. Then again, knowledge of the disability can help the young person understand the source of his or her anger and give him or her more confidence in striving for virtue.

Conversely, underlying behaviours may also work in favour of certain good character traits – for example, a person may be orderly and fastidious, possibly even to excess. If excessive, then it is no longer a virtue, but it could, with adaptation, become a foundation for virtue to take root and grow.

## What character education is

Irrespective of all underlying traits or behaviours, there are good, right, and worthwhile ways of behaving which one would like people to develop. Such good character traits can be learned or developed through practice. They then become habitual, but not in the sense of eliminating individual freedom in action. So, when talking about character education we are talking about assisting in the development of good habits or virtues and overcoming bad habits or vices. Developing such virtue, through practice, is the objective of character education, with the result that a person is better able to master oneself, one's work and one's relationships. For example, good habits such as diligence, sincerity, personal accountability, courage and perseverance are all within a person's reach and can enable that person to develop better relationships and achieve more in the workplace.

The internationally renowned Williams sisters, Serena and Venus, are very talented athletes, but they are particularly good at tennis because they practised the necessary skills, day in day out. Through practice, they developed those skills, which made it easier for them to succeed in tennis. Character growth can be broadly compared to developing such a physical skill, which makes future activity easier. This analogy, while helpful, does not tell the full story. Virtues are not exactly skills, even though they are affected and effected by acts and behaviours. They are more like attitudes of will [and emotion] than skills. Morality is not about being skilful, but about having a good will. Effectively living out that good will, and strengthening it, requires 'skill'/virtue.

Take, for example, punctuality. A person may be a sanguine-type personality; and may lack conscientiousness; but, if helped can learn the virtue of punctuality. This might be done perhaps through bringing home to the person that it is part of the virtue of respect for others – that is, charity; or a persistent effort can be made to attain the habit; or people – e.g. teachers – can insist over a period of time that the person be punctual. In this way, the person can learn to respond well, can develop their punctuality and can have good will in carrying it out in the future. In encouraging good habits it is often better to do so through emphasising the respect for others entailed in the virtue, rather than through a reward system which can promote self-centredness. A young person is also helped by seeing punctuality being lived in the role models around him or her.

## Charity – and also grace – at the heart of it

Reflecting on the challenges of our world helps Christian educationalists to realise that charity needs to be at the heart of education in virtue. Schools cannot make people good but they can put building blocks in place which foster 'goodness' or uprightness or honesty in a student. Our worldly experience of enmity, selfishness and violence highlights the importance of peace and the closely related virtue of charity. Peace in one's heart, in the family and in society begins by developing a 'culture of care.'

For educators to face the personal challenge of inculcating virtue throughout the school day is as important as having a specific programme. The obstacles that prevent us from caring are within us, and the regular reflection and practice of the virtue of charity – of self-giving without seeking reward, of fraternal sharing, of being at peace with ourselves as we are, of interest in others, and of being grateful – can help young people grow in straightforward charity, which in turn is a natural foundation on which the supernatural virtue of charity can be gradually built. Just as learning one's mathematical tables facilitates future mathematical learning, a person who is helped to see and address discord, indifference and selfishness in a systematic way early on is better able to be a sower of peace in later life, should they wish to be.

Despite all that we have said here in highlighting the practical dimensions of character education, it is not the full story with regard to human betterment and human salvation. The goal of a virtuous life is to become like God. To quote St Augustine:

The building blocks of character

> To live a good life means nothing less than to love God with your whole heart and with your whole soul in everything that you do. One who obeys in the same way as the good man would is just; if he meditates on all things in order to avoid deception and lies, he is prudent; if through the virtue of temperance, he gives all his love to God, no trial shall ever overcome him, and that is a sign of fortitude.

Yet we do not save ourselves by our own efforts. We cannot ignore the power and effect of sin and our need of redemption and divine help (grace). We also need to practise the theological virtues of faith, hope and charity, which give life to the other moral virtues. We need forgiveness, divine healing, reconciliation and grace to strengthen all our natural efforts.

Nonetheless, while much of this teaching on the role of the human and supernatural virtues in our salvation is part of the brief of Religious Education, the daily practice of virtue is part of the bread and butter of Catholic schooling. Character education programmes in schools are a whole school task, and for a Christian or Catholic school they are well worth every effort taken. Any success here advances academic excellence, as well as making Christian living a more exciting and realisable challenge. Also, character education programmes can help immunise the curriculum from secular tendencies to some degree, as materialist and relativist worldviews do not sit easy with claims to objective standards – which ultimately lie behind moral character education. Character education can readily be pursued within a secular school environment as well but here also questions must be asked as to the purpose and meaning in life – issues with which Catholic education is very much at home.

Given the central need for character education in modern society, and the help that it can provide in laying a Catholic foundation in schools, some of the steps required for successful character education in schools are outlined at greater length in Appendix 1.

**The power of example**

St. John Henry Newman was aware that liberal education may contribute to a 'noble and courteous bearing' but that it is no guarantee of the formation of conscience. He understood that knowledge in itself did not produce moral effects, so that there must be other means to bring about moral improvement.

When considering college students (at that time in the mid-19th century this specifically meant young men aged sixteen and above), Newman said formation of character was to be achieved by students living together in community, in halls of residence, where the example in virtue provided by senior members, would provide leadership for younger students, therefore helping them to more easily choose the good. The example provided by staff such as the matron, cook or administrative staff had an equally important role to play in that formation. Newman was very aware that 'the young for the most part cannot be driven, but that they were open to persuasion and the influence of kindness and personal attachment.'

Our Irish second-level institutions need to take character formation and moral formation more seriously. Third-level institutions have little interest in it, some mistakenly presuming that the job has already been done. (Employers often complain about the quality of graduates, and often what is missing is that which comes with character education.) Misguided notions of individual freedom abound – where freedom is understood simply as licence, but little attention is paid by authorities in this individualistic age to reminding young people of their community or collective responsibilities. Without such leadership, the weakness brought on by original sin takes over.

Unfortunately, taking the lead from some helpless parents, educational institutions tend to abandon their teenage students to their 'freedoms', at a time when young people still need clear guidance on how to manage their lives. This leaves wide gaps in our civic culture.

The failure of the professional classes in Ireland in recent decades cannot be simply put down to corruption. Commentators seem to always believe that with 'corruption' exposed, things will be different in the future, that somehow or other the coming generation now has resources that the previous generation lacked. It may be that while our educational institutions do cultivate the intellect, they fail the test of conscientiousness, in not educating the whole person. They may be strong in providing facts but are light in providing meaning. Should this continue in our schools, then the new generation of Irish professionals may do no better than the one it is replacing.

## Endnotes

**Character education** – The foremost expert on virtue is German philosopher, Josef Pieper, who over a period of almost forty years (from 1934) collated his thoughts on the cardinal virtues of Prudence, Justice Temperance and Fortitude and on the theological virtues of Faith Hope and Love (Charity). See his works – *The Four Cardinal Virtues* (University of Notre Dame Press, 1990). Also *Faith, Hope, Love* (Ignatius Press, 2011)

**'become like God'** from St Gregory of Nyssa, *De beatitudinibus 1*

**'culture of care'** – see Pope Francis, World Day of Peace message 2021 on www.vatican.va

**Quote from St Augustine** – see St Augustine *De Moribus Ecclesiae Catholicae 1, 25, 46.*

# Chapter 14
# Curriculum: What's on the menu?

> *Key Takeaways*
>
> *The curriculum should ensure that the student understands the great outlines of knowledge and sees the relative value of subjects. All subjects are united in their search for truth.*
>
> *Catholic teachers need additional supports to help explain the Catholic grasp of truth in more depth.*
>
> *The religious education curriculum should educate the intellect and help young people address the serious moral issues they will face, while preparing them for future family life. It should contain a strong emphasis on the reasonableness of the Catholic faith.*

**The modern school**

There are ever-increasing expectations on schools in our society. Apart from an endless series of social objectives that schools are required to subscribe to, the main expectation of the state is that schools prepare citizens for the workplace. The needs of the economy always loom large, with secondary schools now much more structured around the teaching of a wider range of specific subjects at senior level, preparing students for college courses and/or the workplace. Fifteen years ago, the fashion was to teach entrepreneurial skills; more recently the talk is of the need for more science and language learning in *primary* school, as a means of satisfying future workplace demands.

The social expectations on schools are also steadily increasing. Workplace technological advancement does not seem to have lessened demands on parental time and energy. Commuting times for parents of young families have steadily increased; these young families for financial reasons often having to reside at a distance from main employment hubs. Consequently, parents have greater expectations on schools to play an ever greater part in the successful upbringing of their children.

Schools are required to be first responders on a whole range of social issues. They are expected to deal with mental health issues; sexual health questions; alcohol abuse and binge drinking; promote healthy eating and manage eating disorder issues; bullying and cyber- bullying; gang behaviours; drug awareness and drug misuse; coping with stress and exam failure; suicide and copycat behaviours; road safety; managing social media, gambling addictions and combating pornography – part of an endless list on which under-resourced school principals and guidance departments are expected to have expertise. It is quite a challenge to be a first responder, and at the same time seek to be expert in a wide range of academic subjects.

**Curriculum content**

Curriculum is generally understood to be the academic content covered by an educational system. However, in practice it has a much wider scope. It covers the knowledge, attitudes, behaviour, manner, and skills that are imparted to or inculcated in a student. While the curriculum content has its own inherent value – some of which will prove necessary in later life – for the Catholic school the curriculum is also the means whereby young people learn the virtues, values and skills, as well as the graces needed, that will carry them through this world and onto the next.

A well-planned curriculum never loses sight of this final end. Given the now often-conflicting, and indeed constantly changing expectations on schools, it is important that schools themselves would have an overall vision of what education is about, so as not to get dragged hither and thither by current needs or demands, but rather be able to respond fully and appropriately to these real societal needs.

Before setting up the Catholic University in 1850's Dublin St. John Henry Newman delivered a series of lectures which are now contained in a book entitled '*The Idea of a University*'. Much of what he had to say related to people in their late teens, since junior years in university at that time was equivalent to studying for the Leaving Certificate today. Young men of sixteen years of age studied at university for two years, some finishing their education at that point, with others continuing on to specialise in particular professions.

Newman was completely in favour of providing a liberal education for these sixteen-year-olds, drawing on what he himself had experienced as a young Protestant at Oxford. 'Liberal' (in *education*) for Newman was opposed to 'narrowing', such as was brought about through studying only one particular field. For him, a liberal education allowed a student to understand the 'great outlines of knowledge', and to see their relative value. As religion is a genuine part of the study of knowledge, for Newman theology should form part of any course of studies. Through a broad syllabus, Newman thought that one should come to a 'comprehensive view of truth in all its branches, of the relation of one branch of science to another, of their mutual bearings and their respective values'.

Newman was well aware that an educational establishment could never be 'uncommitted'. At a minimum, the selection of knowledge on offer was proof of some commitment. In his mind, being a Catholic need not imply any sinister opposition between the liberal cultural ideal and religion. An institution must teach all it professes to teach unequivocally and without compromise. Catholics, for Newman, had no need to fear knowledge, as all branches of knowledge are connected, 'because the subject matter of knowledge is intimately united in itself, as being the acts and the work of the Creator'.

From Newman we thus capture the idea of curriculum as it should be in a Catholic school. All subjects are united in their search for truth, and therefore interrelated, with the knowledge of the existence of God underpinning all reality. To be true to its mandate the Catholic school then needs to imbue all prescribed curricular material and subject syllabi with this educational outlook, as well as underpinning extra-curricular and co-curricular activity with the value of searching for the good and the true.

Can this be done? As said before, given our constitutional guarantees of freedom and the empowerment in legislation of patron bodies to observe their 'characteristic spirit' or 'ethos', Catholic schools actually have a *duty* to imbue curriculum with this Catholic outlook. In cases where the Catholic outlook is in dramatic opposition to the wider culture this definitely poses challenges for schools, which some schools have successfully addressed. How some of these challenges might work out in the future are discussed in Section 5 and Section 6. The gap between Catholicism and the prevailing wider culture does mean that a Catholic school may need to make adjustments. There are widely available textbooks which a school should decide not to use. Students should never be fed propaganda, be it secular or Catholic. Where textbooks in, say, a subject like History do not give a fair hearing to the Catholic insight into reality this requires a response, rather than acquiescence.

Catholic schools actively promote the sciences, bringing home to young people that the Church has nothing to fear from scientific development, and that the use of science must respect moral laws. The study of philosophy can help people see the correct place of science. Wellbeing classes can help young people appreciate the limitations and dangers associated with communication technology such as cyberbullying or pornography. Helping young people appreciate human sexuality in a Catholic context is one of the biggest challenges facing parents today and schools may have to depend on well-tested international resources to help them in this task, rather than much of the local politicised resources that have been made available.

Too often the job is left to the individual hard-pressed Catholic teacher to navigate the culture and the curriculum, thus often depriving young people in Catholic schools of the necessary ideas and education they deserve. History, English or philosophy teachers may require help in injecting worthwhile Catholic cultural experiences into the curriculum. Regarding the current Junior and Senior Cycle English curricula, many parents and teachers are unaware of the prevalence of NCCA-approved but highly unsuitable literature which normalises hedonistic behavior. Art teachers may need support in showing how the understanding of beauty is a path to God. Science teachers may need to present a short history of science to their students. For example this might remind students that science developed in a specifically Christian milieu, even in the mediaeval ages, due to the fact that Christians see the world as intelligible and knowable, based on the rational nature of the Logos.

In recent years, additional helpful materials have been provided to schools concerning the contribution of women to many areas of learning such as science, literature and politics. Catholic educationalists need to carry out a similar task with regard to the enormous wealth of religious – especially Catholic – influences on our world. Catholic school-supporting agencies need to be much more forward-thinking and organized in providing, and promoting, additional useful resources to schools which explain the Catholic insight into reality and which respect the dignity of young people. Similarly, Catholic schools of education or teacher-training establishments should provide helpful courses and resources to Catholic teachers so that they can help advance Catholic culture within their schools.

## Draft primary school curriculum and its failings

In asking whether it was possible to have a Catholic curriculum, this book answered in the affirmative, basing that answer on the constitutional guarantees of freedom that exist and on the empowerment of patron bodies in education legislation.

The current draft Framework for the Primary School Curriculum, if approved, will turn many of those rights on their heads. It is a Framework which is a proper fit only for secular schools. This curriculum is discussed in more depth in Chapter 17.

## The Religious Education curriculum

All Catholic schools provide a Religion curriculum for their students. The response of a young person to the subject is often related to the attitudes and views that he or she brings from home, and to a lesser extent from the peer group.

Educators should help students to be 'able to give good reasons for their hope', aiming to equip them to become Christian witnesses. A well-structured Religion syllabus educates the intellect and gives young people a valuable understanding of the problems of the world, helps them address the serious moral issues that they will face, while also preparing them for future Christian family life. Pope Benedict, on looking back on his highly successful career as a university lecturer, emphasised the importance of humility on the part of the educator, and of being ready to go along with the other person's insight and to thus help it to mature. Such effective techniques require teachers who can listen and understand as part of teaching.

At primary school level the Religious Education curriculum is in the hands of the patron bodies for the schools. The first-ever formal Religious Education curriculum for Catholic preschools and primary schools in the whole island of Ireland was produced by the Irish Episcopal Conference in 2015. It provides a 'structured outline of what religious education, as an academic discipline in Catholic schools, contributes to the Catholic education and formation of young children at preschool and primary level.'

Under the proposed new framework for primary education this subject will be part of the Religious/Ethical Patron's Programme. As discussed, the wider constraints of the proposed Primary school Framework will pose a major challenge for the adequate implementation of this curriculum.

Drawing on *The Catechism of the Catholic Church* and the vision outlined in *Share the Good News: National Directory for Catechesis in Ireland,* the curriculum has been devised on the basis of the partnership between home, school and parish. According to its foreword,

> the four-fold structure of the curriculum provides a clear scope and sequence for religious learning, with clear signposts to the knowledge and understanding, skills and processes to be learned at each level of the primary school.

These four interrelated strands are Christian Faith, The Word of God, Liturgy/Prayer and Christian Morality.

Strong criticism has been levelled at the deficiencies of the previous primary school curricula and their educational effectiveness. If Religious Education in Catholic schools does not adequately present the mystery of the Blessed Trinity and of Jesus Christ – true God and true Man – to students, then why have such a subject? Teachers of religion should never make the mistake of seeking to dumb down the mysteries of faith to make these more palatable or to try to make the divine more human. The challenges of secular society will never be adequately met by people who have a poor sense of the divine. The new *Grow in Love* series has had no time yet to prove itself, but, as unfortunately happened with previous programmes, it should not take twenty years for Catholic education authorities to uncover or admit to any deficiencies.

According to the NCCA,

the Patron's Programme is developed by a school's patron with the aim of contributing to the child's holistic development particularly from the religious and/or ethical perspective and in the process underpins and supports the characteristic spirit of the school. There are a number of patrons' programmes in the Irish primary school system reflecting the diversity of patronage. ... All patrons' programmes contribute to the child's development and sense of identity and support their connection to community and wider society.

Speaking to educators in 2008 Pope Benedict said:

Catholic schools have the duty and privilege to ensure that students receive instruction in Catholic doctrine and practice. This requires that public witness to the way of Christ, as found in the Gospel and upheld by the Church's magisterium, shapes all aspects of an institution's life, both inside and outside the classroom. Divergence from this vision weakens Catholic identity and, far from advancing freedom, inevitably leads to confusion, whether moral, intellectual or spiritual.

Diocesan education advisers, through the provision of suitable educational materials, have an important role in helping Catholic educators assist young people, and by extension their families, to experience the harmony between faith, life and culture. The wider the gap between the prevailing culture and the Catholic grasp of truth the more important that task becomes. However, as with all education, it is through a unity of vision and an integral approach that young minds will be satisfied.

## Deficiencies in Religious Education at second-level

Second level schools are not obliged by the Department of Education to provide any education in religion. Catholic school patrons are required by diocesan authorities to opt for a school-devised Religion programme (the equivalent to a school subject) or to follow the exam syllabus in Religion. Thus schools can prepare their students in line with the Junior Cycle or Senior Cycle Religion subject or set their own curriculum which is overseen by local diocesan education advisers. About half of students take the Junior Cycle exam subject and around 2% take the Leaving Certificate exam subject.

## Curriculum: What's on the menu?

Anecdotal evidence suggests that the Junior Cycle Religion subject is inadequate in providing an intellectual underpinning of the Catholic faith. Some regard the syllabus as, at best, agnostic. Some schools which don't teach the Junior Cycle Religion subject find it a struggle to provide valuable structured alternatives. A parallel situation persists in the teaching of Religion in senior cycle, with only a tiny minority of students – as indicated above – taking Religion as an exam subject. Irish Catholic education agencies need to provide a confident, Catholic, six-year curriculum and resources which can be adapted and adopted by Catholic schools. This curriculum should include a strong emphasis on the reasonableness of Catholic faith, the basic historicity of the life of Christ, as well as addressing lacunae outlined in Chapter 11, so that schools can properly address the current secular culture in which Catholic faith has first to survive, and then thrive.

According to Dr John Murray of DCU, Catholic schools should not only provide faith development but also reason development:

> Such development of reason will include a confident approach to the God question, which, in light of the Church's championing of reason and its ability to come to know of God's existence as Creator, will be seen as a question allowing of a firm answer drawing not only from faith but also from human reason. Confident theism should be a trademark of every Catholic school, an integral aspect of its ethos.

Certainly this would provide one strong building block for a secondary-school curriculum, but it will require that time is given within the school day for the full duration of schooling, including at senior years.

Major reform of the Leaving Certificate is now overdue. It is likely that any new curriculum in senior-secondary school will contain a 'Wellbeing' or equivalent programme to prepare young people for life. For example, such a programme might include work experience, wellbeing modules, physical education and/or a volunteering credits system, and may need to be given a CAO points allocation to ensure its implementation. It would be imperative that Catholic educators would seek to include the option of, say, an 80-hour Religious Education syllabus for those schools wishing to teach it.

## *Endnotes*

**Regarding the current Junior and Senior Cycle English curricula** - see for example *www.irishparents.blogspot.com* for parental assessments on the NCCA recommended books.

**strong criticism made about the deficiencies of the previous primary school curricula** – see '*A Theological and Pedagogical Analysis of the Catechetics Programme for Irish Catholic Primary Schools 1996-2004*' by Eanna Johnson at http://eprints.nuim.ie/3076/

**Speaking to educators in 2008 Pope Benedict said** – see address to Catholic educators in Catholic University of America 17 April 2008 on www.vatican.va

**Reasonableness of the Catholic faith** – the *So What* series of publications (see *www.sowhat.ie*) includes *God Exists – So What* which shows young people, despite living in a deeply disbelieving culture, how belief in God should be the default position of any young person seeking happiness. Also some of the best-selling writings of Rodney Stark or indeed Tom Holland can help raise sights above the mundane questions such as 'why do I have to do this?'

**Dr John Murray of DCU** – see chapter by Dr Murray in Seán Whittle (ed.), *Irish and British Reflections on Catholic Education* (Springer, 2021). Quotation here is from a summary blog written by the author on www.ionainsitute.ie

# Chapter 15
# Educating in prayer life

> **Key Takeaways**
>
> *Piety – giving filial worship to God as Father – should be encouraged in Catholic schools.*
>
> *This can be facilitated through the school environment and décor as well as with regular practices of piety built into the school calendar, including extra-curricular activity.*
>
> *Catholic schools should encourage people of other faiths to practise personal piety.*
>
> *Schools should help all young people to be open to all that is good and true in the wider culture.*

**A proper objective of a school**

Speaking to educators in 2014, Archbishop Eamon Martin pointed out that 'Ireland shares with other parts of Western Europe a certain loss of the "sense of the sacred"'. While the Religion syllabus aims to educate the intellect, a school needs to look at ways in which it can help students ground their faith in a personal love for Jesus Christ. In this way the Catholic culture of the school seeks to have an influence on piety.

Earlier in Chapter 3, Christians were defined as followers of a person, Jesus Christ. Yet how can one get to know Christ? How can one know someone whose footprints are two thousand years old? The past cannot be recreated. Locating Christ in the history of his time, while useful, is simply inadequate (and perhaps too much emphasis can be placed on this in religious school textbooks.)

Well, just as one needs to use mathematical methods to comprehend the depths of mathematics, a person needs to use religious ways to comprehend religion, and the most fundamental act of religion is prayer. So, while looking at Christ's footprints and also learning from the history and living memory of the Church that He left behind, the best way to get to know the person of Jesus Christ is through prayer. Prayer then is yet another way of knowing, and teaching young people how to pray is thus a proper objective of any Catholic school. As the history of religions show, and as Christ reminded his followers when he instructed them to pray 'Our Father', it is through the community of his Church that we pray and that the past is made present to us.

**What piety means**

This chapter is entitled 'Educating in prayer life'. An alternative title might involve replacing 'prayer life' with the much less regarded but more fitting word 'piety'.

If ever a word had a bad name, it is piety! *Pietas* in Latin means dutifulness – to one's family, country, God etc. It has nothing to do with looking holy, feeling holy, giving the impression of being holy – many of which outward shows are simply hypocrisy. Rather, true dutifulness to family, country and God is a virtue to be upheld.

This proper understanding is best described in the words of Pope Francis

> Piety, therefore, is synonymous of authentic religious spirit, filial confidence in God, of the capacity to pray to Him with love and simplicity which is proper of persons who are humble of heart.

Some elements of popular piety need to be expunged. St. John Henry Newman found certain Italian pious practices rather difficult to take. Some Irish piety can be partially influenced by superstition. Pope Francis warns that certain forms of popular piety can be taken advantage of by people who are not interested in the good of society and the person, for example the forms of piety than can surround inauthentic claims of private revelations.

In seeking to continually purify Irish popular piety, one must be careful not to judge it harshly, conscious of its historical origins. In any such evaluation the words of Pope St Paul VI are apposite:

(Piety) manifests a thirst for God known only to the poor and to the humble, rendering them capable of a generosity and sacrifice to the point of heroism in testifying to the faith, while displaying an acute sense of the profound attributes of God: paternity, providence, His constant and loving presence. It also generates interior attitudes otherwise rarely seen to the same degree: patience, an awareness of the Cross in every-day life, detachment, openness to others and devotion.

So, in the Irish education system, rather than focus on any negative aspects of popular piety, a good starting point might be the words of Pope St. John Paul II when he said that popular piety is a 'treasure of the People of God'. Rather than worry too much about the pejorative undertones and seek to abandon the word piety, teachers should help students come to appreciate the richness of the term.

**The school environment**

A first consideration here must be the school's overall surroundings. There are different approaches to Catholic décor. In the past, religious décor tended to be showy, epitomized by large statues dominating hallways of schools. A less ostentatious piety might be more in keeping with our modern society, given also our increasing multi-culturalism.

The school's Catholic décor should not seek to impose on people's freedom, but it should be present in a declarative and encouraging way. Typically secular institutions which are proud of their ethos mount tasteful and well-thought-out displays of appropriate scale, depending on the location within the building. Reminders of the history and ethos of the institution – by way of photographs and memorabilia – are to be found on office walls and corridors throughout the structure. These secular standards can serve as a guide to interior design in Catholic schools. A crucifix in a classroom, a picture or statue of Mary in a hallway, a May altar in a recess, a sacred space table in a classroom, or a Christmas crib are all helpful ethos reminders for school staff and students.

**Personalising piety**

Where possible, any schoolroom that serves as a chapel should be well kept and tastefully decorated. Where a school has access to the Blessed Sacrament, by way a school chapel or a nearby Church, the custom of visiting the Blessed Sacrament should be encouraged. Showing proper respect for the Blessed Sacrament is a key teaching and learning moment in any school.

A habit of prayer can be encouraged by prayers at fixed moments in the day or by bringing occasional classes to the Church to explain ideas of reverence, of silent prayer, or practices such as the Rosary or the Stations of the Cross.

All Catholic schools should have access to a Catholic priest, who if not formally called a school chaplain, should be an honoured visitor to class groups, or an invited guest on special school occasions. As many clergy do not have any specific training to work in educational institutions it is important that they receive all practical supports needed to make their visits worthwhile. While schools should not seek to place anyone on a pedestal, opportunities should be taken to acknowledge the commitment and dedication of priests and religious, if only to counteract the unjust hostility generated by detractors.

The liturgical seasons give valuable opportunities to cultivate piety. Class groups or individual graveyard visits can be encouraged in November, as can prayers for the Altar List of the Dead. At Christmas, school cribs can be erected and carol services encouraged.

Depending on the access to a Church, Exposition of the Blessed Sacrament can be encouraged on First Fridays or during Church Unity Week and Catholic Schools Week. During Lent, students can be encouraged to pray, practise self-denial and give alms. Arrangements for a Lenten penitential period can be made with the local church. During May, a class might consider making a prayerful visit to a nearby shrine of Our Lady or create a May altar. Whole school community Masses organised in the local parish church should be considered. In secondary schools short class retreats are often very beneficial on an individual level but also in developing class solidarity. When it comes to public piety or public attendance at sacraments, respect for personal freedom would suggest that secondary schools use an invitational approach, despite the possible need for additional staff to manage those who 'opt out'.

Extra-curricular activities also form part of the service provided by a school. In the words of Pope Francis

Catholic schools, which always strive to join their work of education with the explicit proclamation of the Gospel, are a most valuable resource for the evangelization of culture.

Apart from service to each other within the school community, outreach programmes where students care for the vulnerable or the weak are highly commendable additions to a school's mission of service. Such outreach programmes, by reason of their objectives or the time available for them, can also provide greater opportunities for collective or personal piety.

Each Catholic school should seek to promote its Catholic ethos in a spirit of freedom, allowing for the fact that not everyone comes from the same starting point, and that not all its students are Catholics. Managing well those personal needs of students can be a measure of how a school appreciates individual freedom.

Schools should never fall into the trap of presenting the faith as a collection of guidelines or rules, rituals or routines, or merely symbols. Ultimately, while imparting knowledge and the understanding of a Catholic way of life, the school realizes that its work will be effective insofar as the role models it puts forward understand, show respect for and live that ethos.

**Being open to all**

In recent years changing demographics in Ireland has led to most Catholic schools receiving many more people of different faiths and none. It falls to Catholic schools to embrace people of other faiths in a manner consistent with the inclusivity that has always characterised Catholic education. Mutual understanding and respect between all the community in a Catholic school is of vital importance in our pluralist society. Very valuable guidelines have been produced for Catholic voluntary secondary schools which can assist Catholic schools in creating enriching communities that enable all stakeholders to work together regardless of their basic differences. The guidelines indicate that 'a disposition of openness, sensitivity and understanding is important while at the same time holding fast to the characteristic spirit of the Catholic school and the school's Charter for education.' Judgements will always have to be made but, in general, displays of images from other religions, and such expressions of syncretism, are not appropriate in a Catholic school. Having a non-Catholic doing the reading at a First Communion ceremony simply for reasons of inclusiveness shows a lack of understanding of what is important in Catholic life.

**To be Catholic is to be universal**

The very word 'catholic' means 'universal' and a Catholic culture is open to the world. The fruit of a good Catholic education should lead to a deep appreciation of such a Catholic culture for its students while acknowledging the richness – and faults – of the wider secular culture. Some knowledge of the history of the Church and of the world-wide missionary activity of Catholicism should be communicated, and world events such as World Youth Day and World Meeting of Families celebrated. School visitors such as the Missionaries of Charity, Pure in Heart or Lifeworks and the celebrating of events such as Catholic Schools Week also enhance an appreciation of our Catholic culture. A school cannot achieve everything and the cultural fruits will depend on the degree to which the primary educators (parents) and the school work together on the educative mission.

A person's education is not complete on leaving school, so the school also aims to create a desire for ongoing lifelong learning. Thus a Catholic school will place an emphasis on good reading, on the value of theatre, and on debate and on discussion not only to help young people reflect on societal issues but to develop their critical faculties so that they can contribute to the culture surrounding them. It will also propose to students that they keep up the study of their faith, perhaps through online learning or college groups or parish supports. When all is said and done and whatever else is achieved, a Catholic school encourages its students to work hard and study well while helping them to be conscious that it is through their work, prayer life and Christian service that they will primarily be of help to society.

***Endnotes***

**Speaking to educators in 2014** – from an address '*The Catholic School and the New Evangelisation*' to Edmund Rice Trust Annual Foundation in Belfast on 20 February 2014

**'inauthentic claims of private revelation'** – see Pope Francis *The Joy of the Gospel*, 70.

**'The words of Pope Paul VI'** – See *Evangelii Nuntiandi*, 48 (1975) | by Pope Paul VI

**'Popular piety is a "treasure of the People of God"'** – See Pope John Paul II, *Homily at the celebration of the Word in La Serena* (Chile), Libreria Editrice Vaticana, Vatican City 1988, p. 1078.

**Catholic schools, which always strive** … see *'The Joy of the Gospel'* Pope Francis, 134.

**valuable guidelines have been produced for Catholic voluntary secondary schools** – See *Guidelines on the Inclusion of Students of Different Beliefs in Catholic Secondary Schools* (JMB /AMCSS) 2019.

# Chapter 16
# The school as a professional arena

> ***Key Takeaways***
>
> *Schools are professional workplaces which should be encouraging and supportive environments for staff. The school ethos should be the locus of unity within the school community. This requires that school leaders be committed to providing an integral Catholic education.*
>
> *Teacher induction and CPD in the area of school ethos is an important support which should be available to all staff.*
>
> *The ethos should be reflected in all policies and all aspects and activities in the school and should trump all outside influences.*
>
> *Charity, a key part of Catholic ethos, should pervade all relationships within the school.*

## Management's duty to staff

The school is the professional arena where teachers and other education specialists carry out most, if not all, of their educational work. As professionals these are committed to ensuring that all young people benefit from high quality learning experiences in good quality conditions and in schools that play an important role in the local community.

The concerns or complaints that teachers may have as professional educators are manifold, and these are often expressed through their representative bodies (the teacher unions), as well as through subject teacher groups and occasionally through the Teaching Council, the professional body for teachers. Complaints may range from inadequate consultation by the Department of Education or the ignoring of teachers' voices in the drafting of educational policy, to lack of investment in education and school infrastructure, the need for more non-class time to carry out complex non-teaching roles, poor morale in schools, or inadequacies in pay and conditions. Teacher bodies want to be at the forefront of educational reform and innovation while promoting good practice, which are clear signs of their commitment to the needs of young people.

Notwithstanding the fact that many of the flaws within the national education system or those in any particular school may be outside the control of a school's board of management, it falls to the board to provide an optimal environment for teaching and learning. It is worthwhile to briefly focus on the Catholic school as a professional environment and on how all professionals involved can seek to enhance the education of young people and the service provided to their parents.

Catholic education, of its nature, in keeping with its broad objective of providing a holistic education, will always struggle with inadequate resources in seeking to do its best for its students. That said, the holistic spirit is an important source for fundamental values that should underpin all students' educational experiences while providing an encouraging and supportive work environment for staff. It is what should guide and lead everyone in their respective roles as student, teacher, administrative or support staff, and indeed parent, and be the locus of unity within the school community.

Ensuring that this will be the case falls to the professionalism of the usually hard-pressed voluntary board of management and to a school's management staff. Given that there is seldom enough time in the school year to adequately address the many day-to-day crises that may arise, it is well worth while that management bodies seek to take time out to reflect on the implementation of school ethos, and to put in place long-term measures so that it become a major source of school unity.

**Helping people live out the ethos**

The tension between Catholic and secular worldviews will undoubtedly impinge on the school, so it is important that the school community is helped to understand the characteristic spirit better. As with any whole-school objective, there are well-worked structures which can be used to help make that happen. The Catholic Schools Partnership has provided useful templates to help all members of a school community to appreciate and live out the spirit which has imbued the school since its foundation – in some cases, almost two centuries.

School leadership is important in this regard. Boards of management need to give priority to employing principals who fully appreciate what leadership in a Catholic school requires. In our present times, given the clash of cultures between the school and some segments of the wider society, commitment to ethos must rank very high among those holding leadership roles so that other school staff are supported in their task of delivering an integral Catholic education.

Naturally, given the pivotal role of teachers, it is important that each member of the education staff has a full appreciation of the content of education that a school is committed to. This may at time cause tensions, as teachers do not have the mobility they might wish to have within the education system, and they may find themselves in an educational institution where they do not share the ethos. This will be as true of Catholic teachers in multi-denominational or secular settings as it is of uncommitted Catholics in Catholic school environments.

In the current era of volatility around issues such as school divestment it would make sense to facilitate teachers moving around within the educational system, thus helping to respect their conscience rights as well as assisting schools who wish to employ staff who are comfortable with the school ethos. (In discussing teacher mobility it is worth indicating in passing that it would also be appropriate that older teaching staff wishing to remove themselves from the intensity of the educational coalface could find employment elsewhere within the public service.) Any Catholic school with teachers who have negative sensitivities with regard to school ethos should seek to lessen the impact on these teachers, presuming good faith on both sides. The same applies to other-ethos schools.

In pre-employment interviews school management should help prospective employees understand how the ethos impacts on the day-to-day working of the school, and outline this in detail in staff contracts. Teacher induction should also help new employees come to understand how and where the ethos may impact on relevant areas of school curricula. There is an obvious role for third-level colleges providing Continuous Professional Development on matters closely related to Catholic ethos.

**Ethos should be everywhere**

The impact of a school ethos needs to go way beyond that of being solely an employment contract issue, if it is to be a true service to students. The

Americanisation of the Irish workplace in recent years has made everyone more aware of the ubiquity of the idea of ethos, and how the impact of a brand can filter down even into the design of the washroom. Social media and internet interaction has increased awareness of the importance of the small print in the terms and conditions of service. Thus, it should be no surprise that all school policies and practices should ideally be an appropriate fit to the school ethos. So, the quality of all school relationships or the school's discipline procedures, or even, for example, the interaction between school maintenance staff and students should all benefit from the characteristic spirit of the school.

Earlier, it was indicated how an appreciation of character education should be part of the whole school experience of the student. In a like manner, the NCCA has promoted Junior Cycle Wellbeing not only as an area of learning but also as a whole school endeavour. A similar thoroughness needs to apply to the characteristic spirit of the school. It should be experienced in the classroom, in the staffroom, in the boardroom, on the school bus or in the dean of discipline's office. It should be reflected in the way the school assembly is run, in the tone of extra-curricular activities, in the visitors who are admitted to the school, in the enrolment policy, and in the public events that are organised for parents.

School management needs to be forthright in supporting the ethos of the school, realising that it should trump all outside influences. An ethos which is contingent on political interference from outside agencies, be these civic groups, media, staff unions or indeed the political flavours of the month, does not present its students with the protection the ethos has undertaken to deliver. Part of the success of Catholic education is its integral approach, and it relies on constant adherence to the school ethos for its accomplishment.

## Professionalism, and charity above all

Ireland is very fortunate in the calibre of people in the profession and continues to attract and retain high-quality teachers. The teaching profession enjoys high levels of public confidence and trust.

The Teaching Council Code of Professional Conduct for Teachers provides an ethical foundation along with explicit standards of conduct. It describes a vision of what good teaching should look like and encapsulates the fundamental ethics that inform teachers' work. This helps teachers as well as schools to create a high-quality professional environment, appropriate for Catholic education. Over the past decade most Irish schools have developed robust systems to help address challenges faced by students with additional education needs. This evolution demanded that schools be conscious of each individual as a learner, and that teachers be aware and ready to support the individual needs of each student, thus maximising academic and personal development.

This professional commitment to focus on the needs of each individual reflects the capacity for service that has always existed within the teaching profession in Ireland. From an ethics viewpoint this may be expressed in standards of professional conduct, but from a Catholic perspective it can be considered as an expression not merely of justice but of charity – an expression of love of neighbour shown through generosity and helpfulness.

Such practical, professional interest in students and the implied inherent respect for others should epitomise all relationships within and across the school.

**Teachers are learners too**

Some Catholic schools could take a leaf from Educate Together schools who commit themselves to 'support, promote and continually develop Educate Together ethos' and to 'review and refine Continuous Professional Development (CPD) to support implementation of the Ethical Education curriculum'.

There is often a view that ethos, once stated, is then obvious. This may have been the case in the past when the wider culture was specifically aligned with a Catholic ethos, but it is certainly not so today. All staff need and appreciate ongoing inculturation, however this is to be achieved.

Nowadays is not unusual for students in college to unknowingly adopt a wide range of worldviews, not only ones out of step with a Catholic ethos but even out of step with that prevailing in wider Irish society. Thus, students emerging from university training programmes directly into schools do require very specific CPD to help them master their new surroundings and be able to provide the appropriate educational supports that a Catholic school promises to its students and parents. The CPD for a teacher in a Catholic school should include formation in the Catholic ethos and this should be part of the remit of teacher-training programmes. Ultimately, across the education community the goal must be to ensure that new entrants to the teaching profession have the best possible start to their careers. This applies to teachers who may spend their lives working within a Catholic educational ethos, as well as to teachers in other-ethos schools. Just as newly qualified teachers are required to participate in a professional development framework in these first years of service, Catholic-ethos schools need to provide a similar Catholic framework for its employees. The same applies to other-ethos schools also, of course.

**Endnotes**

**Catholic Schools Partnership has provided useful templates** – see www.catholicschools.ie for booklets and ideas.

**very fortunate in the calibre of people in the profession** – The second review of teacher education in Ireland, *The Sahlberg International Review Report on Initial Teacher Education (2012),* as described by the Teaching Council, indicated that 'Ireland was very fortunate in the calibre of people who were seeking to enter the profession, and that teaching in Ireland continues to attract and retain high calibre teachers' (Teaching Council website) – see www.education.ie for full report.

# SECTION 5
# Current challenges to school ethos

Earlier chapters have explored at length the differences that can arise in educational approaches due to differing worldviews. Catholic education starts from a reflection on meaning and purpose, whereas secular education is often primarily built on utility.

Due to the increasing secularisation of wider society many of the challenges now facing Catholic education in Ireland derive from this clash of worldviews. One might have thought that the solution would lie in a 'live and let live' approach – allowing for each worldview to win its own allegiance over time.

Unfortunately the secular worldview has an inbuilt intolerance, and this is evidenced in some of the challenges being discussed in this section. The historical separation of church and state, which sought to keep religion out of the affairs of state and the state out of moral questions is slowly being eroded, as secularism seeks to promote its own state morality. This secular moral outlook, which can properly be described as another belief system, is always evolving, depending on which ideology is dominant, and behind it lies the coercive power of the state.

In several elements of the curriculum the Irish State now insists on the moral norms of this secular belief system. Some groups within the state apparatus have adopted these and given them precedence over other moral worldviews. With these secular norms emerging at a time of political upheaval in western society one can appreciate how half-baked some of these may be when compared with two-thousand years of moral tradition.

Catholic schools are required to stand up for Catholic moral tradition not only to safeguard it, but also to safeguard our democratic traditions as well, which are built on Catholic-Christian norms.

# Chapter 17
# The new Framework for Primary Schools

> *Key Takeaways*
>
> *The draft Framework for Primary Schools is totally at odds with the idea of a holistic Catholic education. If implemented it will depose and eliminate the current denominational system.*
>
> *Making ERB and Ethics a key area of learning will allow it, over time, to become the prevailing characteristic spirit of a school.*
>
> *Prioritising inclusion (as that term is now supposed to be understood) will make it difficult for any school to properly affirm its own ethos.*

**A fit for secular schools**

When asking in an earlier chapter whether it was possible to have a school curriculum which was respectful of the Catholic ethos the answer was in the affirmative. The response was based on the existing constitutional guarantees of rights and freedoms and on the empowerment of patron bodies in education legislation.

The current NCCA draft Framework for Primary Schools, if approved, will turn those rights on their heads. It is a framework which only properly fits secular schools being, as it is, very much in alignment with the secularist ideas expressed in previous chapters. It pays lip service to the idea of denominational education, and seems to be a complete acquiescence to an ongoing demand by some UN agencies that Ireland provide a more secular national school system. The Framework is totally at odds with the idea of a holistic Christian education. It sees the child primarily through a political lens as being an active citizen and adopts a political view of the person throughout – a child of the state rather than a child of a family much less a child of God. One cannot but visualise images of those US social justice warriors observable on our television screens when reading the Framework goals which speak about 'recognising injustice and inequality'.

## Deposing denominational education

Given the predominance of this political view of the person being adopted in the Framework, it would seem appropriate to use the term 'coup' to explain how it intends to depose the current denominational education system.

Firstly, the new Education in Religious Beliefs (ERB) and Ethics syllabi will together become one of the key 'areas of learning' within the new primary curriculum. The proposed unhelpful secular syllabi for these areas of learning are discussed in more detail in a later chapter. The Framework envisages that these will then be incorporated into two of the five primary school curriculum areas, that is, into Wellbeing, and into Social and Environmental Education. This could be viewed as a means of maximising the amount of time available to these syllabi.

Secondly, and conversely, the Framework proposes to reduce the importance of faith-based Religious Education by excluding it from the five main curriculum areas and including it as 'part of children's learning experience'. Since faith-based Religious Education will no longer be a key area of learning, its influence on the wider curriculum will be reduced, while also diminishing the available time for it, leaving it to compete with a range of other extra, unscheduled school activities.

Thirdly, this rearrangement will result in the tenets of secular education as expressed in ERB and Ethics becoming the primary prevailing characteristic spirit, filling, as it will, a substantial element of the overall curriculum and requiring that schools prioritise inclusion.

An emphasis is placed on the need to make all students and families 'feel' included and experience a sense of belonging. By prioritising inclusion over the teaching of religion – as this Framework does – it becomes impossible for a school to confidently affirm its distinctive ethos and endorse its own distinctive set of religious beliefs. Secularists today often use the ill-defined term 'respect' to replace the out-dated but well-defined notion of tolerance. By their definition, a school which affirms its ethos is showing a lack of 'respect' to those who do not share it. In such circumstances anyone who 'feels' excluded, or, even worse, does not 'feel safe' at the expression of such a clear ethos, is obviously experiencing exclusion. This is not an exaggeration – it is simply explaining the language of the belief system to which the Framework hitches its wagon.

Secularism behaves like the bully in the school yard – no one is allowed to express a viewpoint other than the secularist one.

The proposal that the ERB & Ethics programme be taught in all schools is effectively asking schools to adopt a state religion in which commandments are replaced by treaties – ensuring that Caesar not only is given what belongs to him, but that he is also given what belongs to God. The 2020 Programme for Government *'Our Shared Future'* frames the objective in the following way:

> ensure that a curriculum of multiple religious beliefs and ethics is taught as a national curriculum of tolerance and values in all primary schools.

To highlight the stark differences involved, this author may be accused of stretching a point, but the NCCA's single-minded approach to ethos is suggestive of the notion of the State 'endowing a religion', something clearly forbidden under Article 42.2.2 of the Constitution. Even should this overall draft framework not see the light of day there are immediate issues that Catholic schools may need to address with regard to the place of the Patrons Programme, ERB and Ethics under the umbrella of the existing 1999 Primary School Curriculum.

### *Endnotes*

**'part of children's learning experience'** – see page 11 of the *NCCA Draft Primary Curriculum Framework* on www.ncca.ie.

**'feel included and experience a sense of belonging'** – see page 20 of the *NCCA Draft Primary Curriculum Framework* on www.ncca.ie.

# Chapter 18
# Relationships and Sexuality Education

> *Key Takeaways*
>
> *Secular viewpoints on RSE are ever evolving and have no scientific or evidential base to support their claims.*
>
> *The NCCA would appear to have made no attempt to accommodate Catholic insights into reality.*
>
> *The manipulative use of language internationally makes it difficult to evaluate any programme. Despite claims to the contrary, proposed RSE programmes do not derive validity from UN Treaties.*
>
> *It is impossible to teach morality in the moral-free holistic sexuality model currently being promoted.*

**Western society deeply confused about sex**

The Catholic identity of a school extends across all aspects of the curriculum. Where the Catholic identity is in conflict with the wider culture it is important that schools seek to provide the maximum benefit of this Catholic characteristic spirit to students, for this is generally why their families have chosen the school.

At times, the understandings of the wider secular culture and of Catholic culture run almost in parallel. Thus, for example, there is an appreciation across western society of compassion, although the culture's understanding of the word only approximates to the Catholic understanding. Yet, this approximation is sufficient for a Catholic teacher to comfortably compare and contrast both ideas in the classroom and convey the Catholic understanding of the depth of this word.

But the two cultures can also diverge so significantly that there is little to be gained at all from the secularised western culture. This is definitely the case when it comes to the programme for Relationships and Sexuality Education (RSE).

Western society is suffering an ever-increasing confusion with regard to sex, and consequently relationships, whereas Catholic insights in this area has been remarkably stable by comparison. Since the sexual revolution of the 1960s there has been no evolution in timeless Catholic principles, although the manner in which these principles are explained has changed to meet the culture head-on. On the other hand, a review of sex-education literature, even over as short a period as the past decade, displays ever-evolving secular viewpoints, based on the emergence of an increasing diversity of sexual and gender identities and relationships. Even key terminology on sexual identity in the 2019 NCCA report on RSE differs from terminology used in an Oireachtas report which predated it by only six months.

From a Catholic perspective – and indeed from other religious viewpoints – the western confusion about relationships and sex is deeply worrying. A worldview which encourages pornography, which sees abortion up to birth as a liberation, which seeks to ban books which oppose gender-reassignment surgery for children, which is unable to understand or place clear boundaries between friendship and sexual relations, which acknowledges no normative consensual sexual behaviour, which undermines marriage and which promotes gender-fluidity is more removed from the Christian worldview than Roman paganism was during the early centuries of the Church. It only makes sense then that Catholics will closely scrutinise any proposed state curriculum in the area of RSE.

A detailed discussion of such a curriculum is beyond the scope of this book. But it is important to point out the influences underlying the proposed curriculum and the problems that these will cause Catholic schools in the coming years. Resisting such influences are not battles which can be won by a faithful remnant of schools but rather ones which depend on Catholic communities uniting in solidarity around the educational freedoms one would expect to experience in western liberal society.

**Freedom to be different and to do the good**

The primary good to be contended for is that of freedom. Catholic schools seeking to transmit a Catholic outlook should be free to do so. One might think that this would be an automatic right within a free and fair society – but the omens are not good. Whereas modern society noisily demands diversity, and education officials laud school autonomy, these do not seem to be to the fore when it comes to schools making different decisions in the provision of Relationships and Sexuality Education.

On this occasion, yet again, science, however reluctantly invoked, shares the Catholic grasp of truth. International surveys on the effectiveness of existing WHO-promoted RSE programmes on declared measurables – such as whether programmes lead to reductions in unplanned pregnancies and in sexually transmitted diseases or to an increase in teenage sexual delay – indicate little evidence as to their effectiveness. For example, a 2016 major international review of peer-reviewed articles which covered 55,000 students found that the programmes

> had no demonstrable effect on the prevalence of HIV, or other STIs. There was also no apparent effect on the number of young women who were pregnant at the end of the trial.

Such results are not surprising to Catholic educators who have always realised that broader social factors such as one's family, peers and mass media are more persuasive influences than school programmes. They therefore focus instead on the values of personal responsibility.

Undoubtedly any claims by Catholic schools to exercise freedom in running their own programmes will be criticised for going against claimed UN-treaty rights – which are non-existent, since no international treaty explicitly refers to sex education. For example, UN Treaty Implementation groups currently argue that due to the significant range of human rights impacted upon by sex education, it is appropriate to limit the role of religious and cultural norms in the delivery of sex education.

**Legislative threat to freedom**

The 1998 Education Act recognises that the characteristic spirit of the school is an important factor in the delivery of the school curriculum. The Act states:

A recognised school shall provide education to students which is appropriate to their abilities and needs and, without prejudice to the generality of the foregoing, it shall use its available resources to… (d) promote the moral, spiritual, social and personal development of students and provide health education for them, in consultation with their parents, having regard to the characteristic spirit of the school.

At the time of writing there is a left-over Bill from the last Dáil which sought to guarantee in law the right of students to receive factual and objective relationships and sexuality education *without* regard to the characteristic spirit of the school. It also requests that the Minister ensure by law that the curriculum for relationships and sexuality education 'is factual and objective, age appropriate, and not gender normative' and includes among other things 'the different types of sexuality', 'the different types of gender', 'the termination of pregnancy', and that 'the rights of students to access factual and objective education on reproductive healthcare is guaranteed, protected and upheld in schools'.

This Bill clearly betrays the totalitarian nature of those promoting it – that they are ready to set at naught the rights of parents and schools in this regard, and that they feel the need to impose their worldview on all children in the state.

## Applying pressure

Pressure will be applied on all schools to toe the line on whatever RSE programme is officially promoted by the NCCA in 2021. This will most likely be done by integrating the RSE syllabus into a mandated Wellbeing programme for school-children at all levels, and then using the inspectorate to ensure that all modules of the programme are taught. Political activism outside of schools by anyone, be they individual parents, students, teacher unions, other national bodies or interest groups, will be used to force any errant schools to comply with the official wisdom of the wider culture, even though the school still has the defence of 'characteristic spirit' open to it.

## What a Catholic educator might look for in an RSE programme

Much of the language in which the aims and objectives of RSE programmes are couched appears unobjectionable. Terms such as 'respect', 'tolerance', 'fairness', 'positive', 'healthy', 'inclusive', 'age-appropriate', 'holistic', 'values', 'objective-based', 'safe', and 'parental involvement' can be just as equally applied to Christian-inspired programmes as to secular ones, although the secularist definitions will depart from their originally understood meanings. Indeed, at times, it would be fair to classify some of the secular usage of language as manipulative, making, as it does, much of the terminology used unhelpful and uninformative.

What the Catholic educator will be on the lookout for is the overall morality underpinning any topic, a sensitivity to modesty and chastity, an understanding of how young persons' needs for boundaries are fulfilled, and how rights to personal privacy of all students are fully respected. In the words of Archbishop Eamon Martin speaking to Catholic educators in 2018:

> Relationships and Sexuality Education … should present the positive, yet challenging Catholic vision for relationships, chastity, marriage and the family. This will include the Good News that: human life is sacred, that each human being comes from God, who created us, male and female; that we are willed by God who loves each and every one of us; that self-giving love and commitment in the marriage of a man and a woman open to life is not only possible, but is a beautiful and fulfilling gift with the power of God's grace; that chastity is achievable, healthy and good for our young people; that the giving of oneself to another in marriage for life is special, rewarding and a wonderful symbol of Christ's forgiving, faithful love for his Church.

**The political nature of RSE**

The guideline document produced by the NCCA speaks of seeking a shared vision and understanding of what good RSE is, but it falls at the first hurdle. In outlining its overall approach the document says:

> The approach to provision for RSE set out here is grounded in the rights and needs of children and young people as set out in numerous international human rights treaties and instruments that refer to the right to education and to the highest standard of health. These include the Universal Declaration of Human Rights; the UN Convention on Economic, Social and Cultural Rights; the UN Convention on the Rights of the Child; the UN Convention

on the Rights of Persons with Disabilities; and the UN Convention on the Elimination of All Forms of Discrimination Against Women.

These foundational agreements form the basis for comprehensive sexuality education in all countries that ascribe to upholding these rights.

Apart from the fact that the rights to education transcend any international treaties, the actual claim that any specific RSE programmes derive validity from such treaties is categorically disputed by many. In a paper by Curvino and Fischer (2014), the paper's abstract states

> The international community is currently debating whether international law requires States to educate adolescents about their sexuality. Various nongovernmental organizations, United Nations Special Rapporteurs, and treaty-monitoring bodies assert a right to comprehensive sex education, a controversial approach to sex education that arguably encourages adolescents to experiment with their sexuality. This assertion of a right to comprehensive sex education is erroneous and misleading. International human rights are created in two ways: by treaty and by custom. Treaties do not mention comprehensive sex education, or any other form of sex education or training. Custom, found in international consensus documents and other declarations of political will, and confirmed by State practice, holds no universal agreement on sex education. Because neither treaty nor custom creates a right to comprehensive sex education, no such right exists.

As the title of that paper states, claiming a right 'does not make it so.' Even the best of international treaties are negotiated settlements couched in cautious language. Treaties can however be often misused by implementing-committees to promote specific topical secular agendas. The fact is that these treaties have no bearing whatsoever on the RSE syllabus.

**What sort of programme is envisaged?**

The aforementioned article by Curvino and Fischer speaks of a controversial approach to sex education ('that arguably encourages adolescents to experiment with their sexuality') which is now generally termed holistic sexuality education and is the latest model promoted by the World Health Organisation (WHO). This model moves away from the previous model promoted by WHO, which supposedly sought to reduce teenage pregnancy and the incidence of STI, and which, as seen earlier, 'had no demonstrable effect.' By adopting this new model which promotes a 'positive view of sexuality' it is not clear, in the absence of the success of the previous WHO model, if there are any public health indicators which will measure the success of the new model. But it is clear that the new model has taken on board revolutionary new ideas on gender identity and on what is now to be regarded as sexually normative, and seeks to advance viewpoints which are unsubstantiated by medical science itself.

In regard to the impact of compulsory RSE programmes as implemented to date in Ireland, a recent ESRI study reinforces the international findings that there is 'little relationship between receiving Relationships and Sexuality Education or not and young people's sexual behaviour and competence'.

The following are features of the holistic sexuality education which the NCCA is considering:

- It promotes 'sexuality as a positive human potential and a source of satisfaction and pleasure'
- It doesn't aim to prevent young people from starting sexual relationships
- The focus is on behaviour preparation and development (it does not aim to change behaviour).

Even if the content of such a programme were completely innocuous – which it isn't – on the above criteria it would be impossible for any school to place morality into a moral-free, non-judgmental model.

## The content of RSE

The final content of any holistic RSE programme will undoubtedly mirror that of the international programmes promoted by WHO. The normalising of sexual experimentation and of the gender-fluidity ideas underpinning the content of WHO programmes should leave one in no doubt as to the sexualisation effect of these programmes on all of society. Parental concerns expressed by many with regard to the Pandora's Box nature of such programmes are well founded. Ignoring such concerns can only quite properly lead to an ever growing de-schooling movement.

Pope Francis has often spoken of a 'throwaway culture' where humanity has lost any sense of proper human development and worth. For him:

> The book of nature is one and indivisible: it takes in not only the environment but also life, sexuality, marriage, the family, social relations: in a word, integral human development. Our duties towards the environment are linked to our duties towards the human person, considered in himself and in relation to others.

Pope Francis continued:

> it is contradictory to insist that future generations respect the natural environment when our educational systems and laws do not help them to respect themselves.

It might help to take just one of the more redeemable elements of the current RSE programme to clarify some of the points raised here.

A casual approach to sex and alcohol consumption has led to increasing sexual pressure on young women in society. Cases are regularly reported where one person involved in a sexual encounter believed it to be consensual, while the other person believed it to be rape. Thus there has been a recent focus in RSE to make 'consent' the lynchpin and measure of morality for all sexual behaviour.

In the absence of second-level 'consent' programmes, third-level colleges are under pressure to compulsorily educate (or re-educate) all their student body as to the meaning of 'consent'. All these aspects involved in consent (for example, why 'no means no' is not the full story, how consent must be given on every single occasion, how consent cannot be transferred across sexual acts, how to become fluent in the language of consent, the legal system and consent, the danger of misogynistic judgements) give rise to a complexity which could be mostly avoided if the first principles of true self-respect had been previously taken on board.

In abandoning the natural and rather straightforward morality around sex, as espoused by the Christian tradition, secularist thinking is obliged to introduce a new and more complicated morality based solely on legalisms, which is far from complete, and which seeks to impose compulsory education in these legalisms, and which will undoubtedly leave a trail of damaged bodies and minds in its wake.

Certainly 'consent' is an important aspect of RSE but a programme which focuses instead on love and responsibility already fully acknowledges and includes the idea of consent, and sets a very high bar indeed. The Christian approach to sexual morality may make very challenging demands on young people but it is truly more responsive to their present-day needs. Young people seek meaning and purpose and wish to experience love. Rather than being abandoned to manage their conflicting feelings for themselves, they want to hear the truth about the link between love and sacrifice, about what real 'respect' means, and about the importance of reason – even if they also know they may have difficulty in rising to the demands of that truth.

**A proper RSE syllabus**

In the 2016 Programme for Government, in a section entitled *Striving for Excellence in Education*, there was a commitment to developing inclusive and age-appropriate RSE and SPHE curricula across primary and post-primary levels, including an inclusive programme on LGBTI+ relationships and making appropriate legislative changes if necessary. Undoubtedly there will be people who will continue to work to ensure that RSE is taught in line with publicly-available WHO norms. Given that WHO consider RSE as starting in early years and comprising cognitive, social, emotional, interactive and physical aspects and not just the biological facts, it is likely that every clash between the Catholic and secular worldviews on gender, abortion, pornography, sexual identity, family, surrogacy and disability will become areas of contention.

Proper RSE, adapted to the needs of the school, can form an integral part of any Wellbeing programme provided by a Catholic school. Elsewhere, this book has highlighted many Catholic principles that should apply across the curriculum, and these principles also apply to the content of the RSE syllabus. Being true to the truth will require consistency between what is taught in Wellbeing and all other subject syllabi in a Catholic school. And a proper RSE programme cannot simply be a watered-down version of a values-free secular programme. Young people at an early age need to have ideals presented to them, despite how demanding these may look to some. They need to hear about sex and relationships in the context of virtue, especially virtues such as discipline, self-mastery, modesty, respect for others and courage. The place of sex as an intimate expression of human relationships reserved for marriage and the characteristics of friendship relationships are all topics that require age-appropriate inclusion in senior-primary and junior-secondary programmes. Such programmes will also need to be informed by Catholic moral teaching. Serious work is required by Catholic authorities to get this balance right if they are to be faithful servants or stewards and give young Catholics their proper portion of food at the right time. *(St Luke's Gospel, 12:35).*

Catholic parents and Catholic schools should expect their right to be different to be fully respected in a modern democratic society and should not submit to any administrative or political bullying that might be used to bring them to heel.

## *Endnotes*

**Cochrane** published a 2016 major review of peer-reviewed articles covering 55,000 students. See https://www.cochrane.org/CD006417/INFECTN_school-based-interventions-preventing-hiv-sexually-transmitted-infections-and-pregnancy-adolescents

'**A recognised school shall provide education**' – see The 1998 Education Act, section 9(d)

**Catholic view on RSE** – see keynote address by Archbishop Eamon Martin to JMB/AMCSS 31st Annual Conference Galway, 3 May 2018 on www.catholicbishops.ie

**Curvino, M. and Fischer, M. G.** (2014) 'Claiming comprehensive sex education is a right does not make it so: a close reading of international law', *The New Bioethics,* 20(1), 72-98.

**ERSI** – see ERSI '*Talking about Sex and Sexual Behaviour of Young Adults in Ireland*' Nov 2020

For more information on **holistic sexuality education** see *Relationships and Sexuality Education (RSE) in Primary and Post-Primary Irish Schools A Research Paper* Dr. Seline Keating, Professor Mark Morgan & Dr. Bernie Collins. Also see Ketting, E., Friele, M. and Michielsen, K. (2016) '*Evaluation of holistic sexuality education: a European expert group consensus agreement*', The European Journal of Contraception and Reproductive Health Care, 21, 68-80.

# Chapter 19
# Wellbeing

> *Key Takeaways*
>
> *The principles of the Junior Cycle Framework are compatible with Catholic education.*
>
> *Many of the areas under Wellbeing can benefit from the Catholic insight into reality. Currently there is an over-emphasis on personal autonomy at the expense of self-giving and the common good.*
>
> *Many areas of Wellbeing would be better delivered within a character education framework leading to less public intrusion into students' personal lives and less narcissistic reflection by students.*

**The Junior Cycle Framework**

The inclusion of non-academic learning opportunities within the school curriculum should generally be welcomed by those who appreciate the Catholic holistic model of education. Those who don't are likely to be those who have a purist sense of the purpose of schooling and may not appreciate schools departing from strictly academic disciplines. But expectations on schools have changed. The demands on modern family life reduce the time available for parent-child interaction, and therefore schools are expected to carry out their 'in loco parentis' role – in the place of parents – to a greater extent than in the past. Schools should seek to carry out this task in a familial way – all students being equally loved but perhaps accepting also that they may receive different treatment.

Unfortunately, the 2015 Junior Cycle framework (the education curriculum for 12-15 year-olds) appears to depart from the holistic model as espoused by Catholic schools and as acknowledged in the 1998 Education Act. In outlining eight principles that underpin the Framework for Junior Cycle – and thus informing its planning, implementation and development – it is acknowledged that the student experience should contribute 'directly to their physical, mental, emotional and social wellbeing and resilience.' Key elements of the Catholic holistic model – such as 'spiritual' and 'moral' – are not included.

The Junior Cycle Framework also outlines twenty-four statements of learning which should shape the curriculum. These highlight many of the expected key learning outcomes for students including communication skills, creativity, understanding of citizenship, and valuing the role and contribution of science and technology. These, however, *do* include ensuring the student 'has an awareness of personal values and an understanding of the process of moral decision-making' and 'appreciates and respects how diverse values, beliefs and traditions have contributed to the communities and culture in which she/he lives'. All this can certainly be understood in a way compatible with Catholic education, but one can see that the principles have been written so as to be more in keeping with a relativistic outlook and a pragmatic view of education, which is seen as a means of acquiring information and achieving personal success.

**A reduction in school autonomy**

That being said, with the initial launching of the framework there was great enthusiasm to give each school its own freedom and autonomy to work within broad guidelines, with Irish, English and Mathematics being the only compulsory subjects in the curriculum, and allowing schools to develop some short courses across all of the curriculum. Yet, in a last minute change, with very little discussion, a new subject, Wellbeing, was included as a compulsory subject. How flexible this obligatory subject will prove to be in respecting the characteristic spirit of schools should now be a matter for active discussion among Catholic educators, given all the headwinds around issues such as objective morality, decision-making, rights without responsibilities, self-autonomy, body image, self-identity and woke thinking.

At primary level, where a new draft Framework is under discussion, Wellbeing is identified as one of five major curriculum areas. Its close identification with ERB and Ethics programmes suggest that adapting it to the Christian worldview will be significantly more difficult than at secondary level, where greater scope for adaptation is currently available. The draft primary school curriculum is the subject of a previous chapter (Chapter 17) and the specific matters of ERB and Ethics curricula are explored in more detail in an upcoming chapter.

## Linking wellbeing and character development

The Wellbeing concept is one which has crept into education in the last fifteen years in response to reports of increased mental and emotional needs of children and young people. Wellbeing programmes are infused with ideas related to (a) emotional wellbeing such as confidence, happiness, feelings of depression; (b) social wellbeing such as relationships, violence, delinquency, bullying, social media usage; and (c) psychological wellbeing such as problem-solving, personal autonomy, and resilience. Intangible terms such as 'social and emotional literacy', 'social and emotional learning' and 'social and emotional intelligence' are also widely used. Wellbeing also looks at the person as an active citizen, and includes such diverse areas as physical education and career guidance. Physical education hours constitute a substantial portion of the Wellbeing syllabus. There are six Wellbeing indicators against which students can measure themselves – these being 'active', 'responsible', 'connected', 'resilient', 'respected' and 'aware' – the focus here being on students reflecting primarily on how they feel about themselves and their circumstances, with not enough attention being given to the part the person plays in wider society, or in responding to the needs of others. Paraphrasing an idea of Pope Benedict: from our very beginnings we are a person 'from others', we live our lives 'with others', and we live our lives 'for others'. Such thinking must infuse any Wellbeing syllabus, if only to counter any narcissistic tendencies that it may otherwise engender.

There are obvious dangers that, because of the need to feel relevant or up-to-date, programmes will promote untested and unproven psychology. So, while the general notion of Wellbeing is welcome in seeking to address the many social and personal challenges young people face today, Catholic educators should give a fuller consideration to the content of Wellbeing and the pedagogical methods used. The failure of past drug education and sex education programmes are strong reminders that education isn't simply about the imparting of information, or knowing more things about issues.

There is a strong case to be made that many of the objectives of Wellbeing can be achieved through modules delivered under the wider mantle of character education at both primary and secondary level. For example, modules on the virtue of cheerfulness would be a very natural way of addressing issues around personal confidence and bullying as well as being a suitably indirect approach to the promotion of positive mental health. Focussing on positive virtues and how to live them, are very natural ways – as they build on the young person's natural optimism and desire for challenges – for teachers to help young people be aware of the struggles to be faced in life. Rather than promoting too much – and often unhelpful – semi-public introspection in the classroom on personal matters of mental health or on family circumstances, a focus on teaching virtue is less intrusive, less self-centred and less narcissistic, and helps the student be more outward looking, seeing himself or herself as part of a community. This is not to dismiss the real-life mental health issues which particular students may face. In fact, it may also help to reinforce a realisation that for many young people such personal issues are frequently better addressed through one-on-one or small group mentoring than in the classroom.

Wellbeing can be a Trojan horse for a secular culture which promotes personal autonomy at the expense of community participation or it can be infused with character development and Christian values throughout. The latter approach will take work, however, as this is clearly not the foundation on which the Wellbeing programme was built.

# Chapter 20
# ERB and Ethics programmes

> *Key Takeaways*
>
> *Compulsory ERB and Ethics programmes will undermine the integral approach of Catholic schools to education.*
>
> *ERB claims that it is neutral but, in fact, it is agnostic. Catholic schools will be constrained from affirming the unique importance of their religion.*
>
> *The Ethics programme seeks to empower the individual at the expense of the common good.*
>
> *Catholicism sees itself as helping people to discover truth; the Ethics programme sees people as developing their own truth.*

**Disregarding Catholic insights**

As previously mentioned, aside from the more traditional academic subjects and the Patrons Programme, a new Wellbeing and Social and Environmental Education programme will form a key part of the curriculum in the proposed new Primary School Framework. New curricula for ERB and Ethics are to be included, with the Framework strongly endorsing these and indicating that these subject specifications will play an important role in the curriculum. This approach, and the compulsory nature of these subjects, will completely undermine the required integral approach Catholic schools have towards education.

Some people, especially those with a limited functional view of education merely as instruction, view the attendance at a Catholic school differing from other schooling models only in terms of the formation given in Catholic doctrine and piety – and with this almost exclusively happening within the Religion class. That would appear to inform the limited view of the NCCA when one compares the principles underlying its ERB and Ethics curriculum with Catholic educational principles.

Much of the discussion in the earlier chapters on the differences between a secularist worldview and the Catholic insight into reality is mirrored when the ERB and Ethics subjects are contrasted with a Catholic approach to religion, ethics and morality. Given that some Catholic groups had made significant submissions on the draft Framework highlighting these real difficulties for Catholic schools, the overall approach of the NCCA could be construed as an attempt to disregard the Catholic insight.

**Education about Religions and Beliefs**

The ERB programme is an unsuitable programme for a Catholic school. The programme claims to provide objectivity, while at the same time the NCCA correctly acknowledges that no subject or teaching is value free.

As the programme presents the claims of each religion as equally true it is essentially denying that any religion is in fact true. It claims that this is a neutral stance, whereas it is an agnostic stance with regard to the existence of any truth. Theoretically, the programme could be presented without examining the truth claims of the various worldviews, but, in fact, to fulfil its objectives it must degenerate into accepting that all religions are make-believe. The programme also envisages students generating their own meaning and knowledge.

A commonly used word in modern woke parlance is a word which we discussed earlier, that is, 'respect'. Until recently people have exercised freedom on the basis of tolerance of others. A healthy tolerance appreciates there will be disagreements among people in views and attitudes – it is an acceptance of the other person's right to be different or to express a viewpoint contrary to our own. Thus, it allows disagreement with dialogue, and acknowledges the right of a person to express views which he or she believes to be true.

In modern woke thinking this word 'tolerance' is being replaced by the new, and now ill-defined, word 'respect'. The new meaning of 'respect' implies responding to the other person's viewpoint in a way which would not lead that person to be offended. This understanding of the word serves as a strong impediment to robust discussion. Thus the more a school affirms its religion as uniquely important the more likely it is that such affirmation could be regarded as lacking in 'respect' for other religious viewpoints. Furthermore, the approach of 'respect' or of 'valuing' other beliefs often requires the celebration of a student's beliefs or non-beliefs (which also include moral outlooks).

Simply expressed, the programme is based on a pluralist idea that there is no way of knowing objective truth, and thus all religions and beliefs are equally 'true'. Nowhere does it acknowledge the concept of objective truth in matters of religion, a view which is held by all Christians and shared by peoples of other religions. The Christian position is that of respecting the person while perhaps not agreeing with the viewpoint the other person might express. To take a historical example, a religion which promotes human sacrifice, or a modern one, a cult which worships the self as God can never be respected, whereas one can understand how individuals could be caught up in such dead-end thinking. This understanding allows for charitable dialogue in the search for truth.

Should the ERB programme be taught in Catholic schools then, in one class students are hearing that all religions are equally true (or false), and in another class (under the Patron's Programme) that the Catholic religion is the one true religion. Leaving aside the disservice to children involved in this, such an incompatibility in curricula fails even at a basic pedagogical level.

That is to read the ERB proposal in its most positive fashion. What ERB really teaches in fact is that these religions are not true! This applies especially to any religion that makes a claim to know, for example, that God the Creator exists, and to know this not only by faith but by reason. By ERB teaching that God's existence is unknowable, it is implicitly teaching that Catholicism is wrong, and that all religions are not equally true. Its position is not coherent.

Catholic schools worldwide attract a wide variety of non-Catholic students. These students' families appreciate the inclusive nature of such schools, while accepting the right of Catholic schools to teach in line with Catholic beliefs. Even some who do not accept Catholic beliefs realise the immense wisdom that accumulates from the Catholic tradition. The truth of the divinity of Jesus Christ is the overarching view through which religion and all other subjects are taught. This right is denied by requiring a Catholic school to teach the ERB syllabus.

**Ethics**

As discussed throughout Section 2, the Catholic understanding of truth is directly at odds with the secular liberal worldview. When it comes to personal moral issues, secular liberalism does not accept the existence of objective truth. In denying God, it provides a worldview which is anchored in the individual making their own sense of the world for their own benefit, developing their own truth. According to the NCCA,

> Ethics education contributes to the development of autonomous individuals, capable of exercising critical judgement, while also fostering dialogue and community life in a pluralist society.

With such ethics, first comes the individual, and the community comes a distant second, and only insofar as it does not impinge on the individual's moral choice. Even the word 'person' is avoided, and the word 'individual' is used, possibly because person is redolent of a particular objective worldview.

Christians, as mentioned earlier, see themselves as persons-from-others, persons-for-others and persons-with-others, understanding that the wellbeing of all, including oneself, is achieved through seeking objective truth and goodness.

Catholics recognise that it is neither praxis – an idea translated into action – nor actions themselves that creates truth but rather that truth serves as the basis for praxis. Or as Pope Benedict expresses it,

> the Church never tires of upholding the essential moral categories of right and wrong, without which hope could only wither, giving way to cold pragmatic calculations of utility which render the person little more than a pawn on some ideological chess board.

The difference between this Ethics programme and Catholicism could not be starker. For Catholics there is objective truth, there is right and wrong which is knowable. The criterion of judgement is not the self: there is something definitive beyond the individual, and there is a requirement to see oneself in others. These ideas are all strangers to the Ethics programme. Leaving the final word with Pope Benedict:

…. When nothing beyond the individual is recognized as definitive, the ultimate criterion of judgment becomes the self and the satisfaction of the individual's immediate wishes. The objectivity and perspective, which can only come through a recognition of the essential transcendent dimension of the human person, can be lost. Within such a relativistic horizon the goals of education are inevitably curtailed. Slowly, a lowering of standards occurs. We observe today a timidity in the face of the category of the good and an aimless pursuit of novelty parading as the realization of freedom. We witness an assumption that every experience is of equal worth and a reluctance to admit imperfection and mistakes. And particularly disturbing, is the reduction of the precious and delicate area of education in sexuality to management of 'risk', bereft of any reference to the beauty of conjugal love.

## *Endnotes*

**Some Catholic groups** – see for example contribution by Rev Prof Eamon Conway, Dr Kerry Greer, Dr John Murray, Dr Rik Van Nieuwenhove, Anne Hession, Dr Thomas Finnegan in
https://ncca.ie/media/2827/erb_ethics_submissions.pdf

**Pope Benedict two quotes** – both these are from the previously mentioned remarks at a Meeting with Catholic Educators, 17 April 2008 –by Pope Benedict XVI in Catholic University of America in Washington. Available on www.vatican.va

# Chapter 21
# When education becomes political

> **_Key Takeaways_**
>
> _Western culture is adopting a view in which everything, including the personal, is now political – this leads to the reduction of the human person to being simply an active citizen. As a result at the present time, education reform – be it about curriculum content, pedagogical methods or institutional structures – is liable to be dominated by political worldviews._
>
> _Woke thinking is a puritanical unforgiving intolerance of humanity's inadequacies which often proposes totalitarian solutions. It undermines all freedoms, including those on which democracy depends._
>
> _Catholic schools must resist woke thinking at every turn. This includes refusing to see life through the politicised lens of sexuality. The Catholic school ethos is empowering in this regard, whereas secular education systems have much fewer effective defences._

**The climate in which reform is happening**

In very recent times in the Western world the growth of intersectional politics and the philosophy of critical theory have had widespread ramifications, not least in tainting all of life with political action. The idea that you might be stopped from making a livelihood because of your political viewpoint or that you might be publicly ostracised for this, reeks of a totalitarianism with which most people today in Western society have not been familiar, and displays the dangers inherent in politicising everything.

When educational reform is being undertaken in such a political climate then an infection of education content and of the educational process becomes highly likely. The new Framework for Primary Schools indicates such influences. For example, it talks of the individual but not of the person, of society but not of the family. One of the key competencies or capacities which the curriculum seeks to build is 'Active Citizenship' which, among other things 'helps children question, critique and understand what is happening in the world within a framework of human rights, equality and social justice' – but not within a framework of objective morality. This competency 'places democratic practices at the centre of the learning process' – a strong echo of the controversial idea of the democratic school in which democracy is both a goal and a method of instruction.

**Active citizens**

Such overt politicisation is also part of the 2020 Programme for Government in its 'commitment to establishing a Citizens' Assembly on the future of education at primary and secondary level.' Leaving aside any inherent criticisms one might have of the possible misuse of such a consultative process within a democracy, what is of more concern is the intersectional approach which the Government proposes to adopt – since the purpose of this proposed Assembly is 'to ensure that the voices of young people and those being educated are central.' Such an intersectional approach will ensure that the many other central voices which need to be heard are not heard, since their views might not lead in the direction of desired outcomes.

The role of education in supporting the development of active citizens for a democratic society is not new, and is a vital part of learning. It is important that students value what it means to be an active citizen, with rights and responsibilities in local and wider contexts.

But enabling young people to develop the capacity to act in democratic societies is not a ground for the democratisation of educational content, of learning methods or of the institutional structures within which young people learn. The way to combat a lack of engagement in political life – as evidenced by individualism in society, or the decline in social capital, or the perceived apathy of young people in relation to social and political life – is not through the increased politicisation of everything but by better providing young people with a sense of purpose and meaning, something which western society has lost sight of over the past two generations and which a thorough Catholic education can provide.

**A new intolerance sweeps across Western society**

In the early 20th century Marxism and Catholicism seemed at a superficial level to have something in common as both addressed inequality in society. But as history now testifies that commonality was not even skin deep. Those who were uncertain then are now fully aware that atheistic materialism is probably as far away as you can ever get from Christian love.

A similar initial confusion is evident between woke thinking and Christianity. Being aware of the importance of social justice, especially with regard to racism, is a very good thing. But any overlap between being woke and Catholicism stops there. Woke thinking moves off then into puritanical intolerance with underlying shades of new Marxist thought, leading to fruits of uncontrollable resentment, divisiveness and violence. Indeed, when examined close up, woke thinking is a parasitical ideology which exploits good human inclinations and leads its adherents towards unworkable anarchical solutions.

Woke ideology proposes that we have messed society up so much that we need to throw out everything – including even our history of past events – and begin again. Its intolerance is much like that of William Roper in Robert Bolt's film '*A Man for All Seasons.*' Some of Bolt's dialogue is worth repeating:

> **William Roper:** 'So, now you give the Devil the benefit of law!'
>
> **Sir Thomas More:** 'Yes! What would you do? Cut a great road through the law to get after the Devil?'
>
> **William Roper:** 'Yes, I'd cut down every law in England to do that!'
>
> **Sir Thomas More:** 'Oh? And when the last law was down, and the Devil turned 'round on you, where would you hide, Roper, the laws all being flat? This country is planted thick with laws, from coast to coast, Man's laws, not God's! And if you cut them down, and you're just the man to do it, do you really think you could stand upright in the winds that would blow then? Yes, I'd give the Devil benefit of law, for my own safety's sake!'

## What it means to be woke

Woke thinking, the political movement of our time, has crept up on many of us, following on from a generation of postmodernism, gender studies and critical theory in our universities. It derives from a vision of society, seen as comprising disparate groups of people. A group is constituted by those who share similar characteristics, such as race. Much like Marx's binary of proletariat and bourgeoisie, all groups are in an oppressor-oppressed relationship with each other. Intersectionality, this division of society into opposing groups, becomes the lens through which all politics is viewed.

By focussing on the *differences* between people, this political theory proposes that all such difference (e.g. of gender, race, colour, ethnicity) is a cause of discrimination. This effectively divides society up into opposing binary groups of oppressor versus the oppressed or victims, making almost everything political. Groups then continue to multiply: a person may be in many overlapping groups, and it is only through victimhood that the individual is provided with a platform to speak. Intersectionality denies an oppressor a right to a publicly expressed viewpoint, increasing any underlying polarisation that might exist, leaving it almost impossible for wider society to address issues – such as racism – through the normal political discourse on which a democracy relies. Deep differences – where these exist – can no longer be addressed through a free exchange of views.

**Everything comes to be about politics**

One of the overriding impacts of modern woke thinking is the politicisation of everything, including what is personal. Workplaces, especially those of multinational companies, have become deeply politicised. Staff are required to implement 'diversity and equity' policies unquestioningly as to query this is taken as an overt expression that you are against diversity and equity. People fear to express what might be perceived as contrary viewpoints as censorship and deplatforming are commonplace and loss of employment can often occur. It is now not unusual – at least in the US – to hear that a commercial company had cut ties with a supplier or customer over an issue of political perception. Maybe the supplier or customer had expressed an unguarded viewpoint, or one which, for some reason, was not acceptable to woke thinking.

This woke culture is now commonplace in Irish universities and seeping its way into the Irish school system. Catholic schools need to adopt a firm stance if they are to ensure that their capacity to promote their characteristic outlook is not emasculated. The insidious, divisive style of woke thinking is destructive of the sense of unity which a Catholic school seeks to generate around its characteristic spirit.

## The corrosive effects of being woke

The difficulties which woke thinking presents are best understood by looking at some of its impacts. Firstly, there is political correctness – the avoidance of forms of expression that are perceived to exclude or marginalise individuals or groups. This creates barriers, hindering people from expressing themselves freely, leaving ordinary people feeling inhibited around ordinary everyday workplace or personal exchanges, not knowing whether the view they might express might be deemed or perceived to be harmful by others. Woke thinking allows speech, at times, to be defined as violence.

This approach in turn has led progressive academics to support placing limits on free speech. For such thinkers, the new liberal causes they espouse are higher goods than the right to hearing opposing viewpoints in the public square. If you don't 'respect' – that is, in its redefined meaning – or possibly even 'celebrate' the opposing viewpoint then you should be censored. The most recent restriction to emerge from academia is a cancel culture or no-platforming approach, operated by radical progressive voices, with the aim of denying space in the real and virtual public square to those opposing 'progressive' viewpoints. All restrictions like these come at a cost, as dissent is driven underground and political resentment grows among those dispossessed of the right to free speech. And without proper political debate no democratic societal progress can be made.

There are numerous corrosive effects of intersectionality impacting on everyday lives. These include: people being physically attacked or being demonised on social media because they are seen to represent the oppressing group; accusations of micro-aggressions; demands for book burning or the denial of book publication; requirement for safe spaces and trigger warnings; widespread misuse of abuse terminology such as 'racist', 'homophobe', 'fascist', 'white-privilege'; over-emotional and irrational responses to perceived, and possibly non-existent, aggression. Woke thinking is a new puritanism in that it allows no forgiveness and seeks to drive all non-woke ideas to the margins.

While not initially identified as part of a woke cultural trend, the anti-Catholic narrative in today's Irish society shows similar characteristics. Society can all agree that it is acceptable for people who break the law or who deliberately undermine or destroy trust to be held accountable. Nonetheless that never makes it acceptable that whole groups within society, for example, those who proudly identify as Catholic, be made somehow responsible for the mistakes of others of yesteryear, often more than two generations ago. Thus, as with woke culture, the unacceptable past of others determines that their 'successors' today are demonised and denied space in the public square.

As woke thinking works its way through society, Catholic schools need to have the tools – and to be able to use them – to help staff, students and parents confront this political culture. One's initial instinct, in the face of such hostility, can be to go along with it for a quiet life. This indeed is one way that woke culture has successfully pushed its way through the institutions. But acquiescing to the bully won't address the educational challenge faced when one is regularly requested to show more 'respect' for difference, agree that unacceptable behaviours are now normative, manage appropriate gender pronouns or continually acknowledge one's own unconscious bias which results from some to-be-uncovered privilege.

**How Catholic schools can keep woke thinking at a distance**

Stories of the disturbing impact of woke culture on American high schools are now emerging. It can impact on course content, especially on the reading material in English and History curricula, or the use of language in Science curriculum. It can, as highlighted below with regard to the state of Oregon, impact on the pedagogical techniques used in various subjects, especially on methods in measuring progress in learning. But more disturbingly it can impact on students' own self-image, particularly around matters of race. Students then resort to saying things to please their teachers, to avoid ostracisation and retribution. By the time their college education comes around students are used to self-censorship. True education can only happen in an atmosphere of freedom, not one of indoctrination. Woke schools do not provide that climate – Catholic education does.

There are some educational approaches appropriate to a Catholic school which, if properly implemented and understood, can help free people from the intolerance of being woke. These include:

- In a Catholic school everyone is accepted for who they are, in their fullness as created persons and are not addressed in relation to particular characteristic improvements. It is easy to pick out faults in society: it is much harder to rectify them. Totalitarian intolerance is not a solution for anything.

**Providing a genuine 'safe space'**

A student grows with his or her school. Within its characteristic spirit the school seeks to allow the student to grow to maturity. As the joys, the interests, the concerns and the fears of students are ever present, in today's climate a school should seek to provide its own political safe zone for all its students. That zone is one in which the personal does not become the political.

Discussion, public speaking and a vibrant exchange of ideas that are in the public forum should be plentiful in a school, particularly at senior level, not least as part of students' learning to develop their own critical skills. Young people should understand their right to speak freely. Despite woke thinking, this can come about by not allowing any politicisation of the school space. There should be no politically-motivated partisan posters, no intersectional groups, no lobbying, no political 'weeks' within the school zone and indeed no student strikes, no matter how laudable the political cause. Even the textbooks used in the school should respect the political safe zone that the school wishes to provide for its population.

Yes, a school will have to address many issues around difference. It can successfully do so by not drawing attention to difference but by showing that everyone is treated as a person, worthy of full dignity by virtue of that fact. While it may be the reverse of the politicisation that is taking place outside of the school, this approach does help to secure a genuine safe space for growth. By severely reducing the possibility of political bullying occurring within the school, true bullying will be more easily identified when it does occur, and then it can be dealt with.

Groups external to the school, including at times even the Department of Education, must be helped to appreciate that students are not a captive audience for them to access but are young people for whom the school takes its *in loco parentis* responsibilities seriously. Currently, the Department of Education has welcome guidelines which acknowledge the power of school authorities and management boards to manage the access outside agencies have to schools. Such responsibilities of management boards should be wisely exercised for the good of all school families.

It may be that, in due course, the current wave of political woke thinking may collapse under the weight of its own foolhardiness – although this is less likely in the short term given forty years of steadily laying down roots. But in the meantime, schools themselves need to be safe spaces for their students. Some of the above principles might need to be outlined in the school's code of behaviour – encouraging students to be proud members of the school community, the school being a politics-free space. Thus, only outside speakers who genuinely respect the school ethos should be invited. No special treatment should be accorded to any group within the school, and people should be respected for who they are.

As a Catholic school, parents should also be helped appreciate the Catholic understanding of what is sometimes termed 'the book of nature', and seek to avoid politicisation of the school in that regard. Thus the school's visible and invisible curriculum on gender, on sexual difference, on relationships, on sexuality, on marriage, on caring for creation, on concern for the poor and on conscience should be in line with Catholic thinking, using the characteristic spirit of the school as a shield to avoid all politicisation of these issues or pressure from external groups. Unfortunately, as society increasingly fails to separate the personal and the political, schools will need to work harder in order to do so.

**Keeping politics out of the curriculum**

Adopting a Catholic ethos allows a school to embrace all that is good in society, while giving individuals the tools to properly question and understand all that is novel.

In the pedagogical methods used to teach traditional school subjects there is *currently* no significant difference on a practical level between schools committed to a Catholic ethos and ones operating with a secular ethos. However, those committed to a secular ethos are more vulnerable to political trends.

For example, in the US state of Oregon, public schools are now asked to view the teaching of Mathematics through a political-cultural lens, which leads the education authorities there to make the following considerations and recommendations:

- There is a need to deconstruct racism in mathematics: 'White supremacy culture infiltrates math classrooms in everyday teacher actions' and thus 'perpetuate(s) educational harm.'

- Examples of classroom actions that perpetuate white supremacy include asking students to show their work, focusing on getting the right answer, tracking student success, and grading students. Such actions must be discontinued.

- For example, asking students to show their work is a crutch for teachers to understand what students are thinking. This is considered white supremacy because it reinforces 'paternalism' and 'worship of the written word.' Worship of the written word is a foundation of white supremacy culture, which reinforces documentation and writing skills.

- Or for example, a Math class that focuses on helping students to get the right answer perpetuates white supremacy. Calling answers 'right and wrong' perpetuates objectivity, which is a tenet of white culture.

Whereas many people may be dissatisfied with assessment methods which solely measure achievement and not effort, yet there is within Catholic pedagogy a clear understanding of what 'excellence' might be in any particular field of studies. This understanding has the capacity to withstand most politicisation of teaching methods. Another example of such politicisation is the view of a US university professor from Arizona State University that any grading of literacy is unacceptable. This professor claims:

> ..(A)ll grading and assessment exist within systems that uphold singular, dominant standards that are racist, and White supremacist when used uniformly. This problem is present in any grading system that incorporates a standard, no matter who is judging, no matter the particulars of the standard.

He later added:

> In our current society and educational systems, regardless of who you are, where you came from, or what your intentions or motives are as a teacher, if you use a single standard to grade students' language performances, you are directly contributing to the racist status quo in schools and society.

Intruding politics into schools' attempts to address inclusion is another area where new woke politics threatens to undermine education values as commonly understood. Teachers currently operate with some ideal standards in mind when they educate. The degree a student's learning approaches such a standard of excellence the better that learning is. Woke culture argues that for disabled students or marginalised students this creates a focus on overcoming 'deficits' instead of focussing on the systemic influences that marginalise and exclude particular groups of students in the first place. Such thinking proposes that it would be much better for schools to adopt a social justice approach and for educators to address education practices that perpetuate inequalities in schools based on power, exclusion and disability.

It is easy to see how subjecting education to such a social justice perspective can lead to an undermining of any standard. The message is as it was in the Oregon example: if standards derive from unjust hierarchies then obviously we cannot depend on them without perpetuating injustice, and so must abandon them. Such views are currently promoted in some material appearing on the Teaching Council website.

Secular education systems are much more vulnerable than truly Catholic ones to politicisation and experimentation in education. Five years ago, one would never have thought that the hidden curriculum in Irish pre-schools would seek to 'challenge' children – especially boys – who build gender boundaries in play, while supporting the boys who cross those boundaries. An educational case can be made for such an approach but it derives primarily from a worldview which regards gender identity as a social construct. Yet this educational approach has developed almost by stealth, without any public discussion of its impact. In a similar fashion, within five years, it is highly possible that a politicisation of Irish schools could lead to approval of some of the unsubstantiated, wild educational assertions currently acceptable in the Oregon State education system or Arizona State University as listed above. In the past, new educational thinking generally required that it be substantiated by empirical proof of its effectiveness – now, in a woke society which approves of the silencing of dissenting voices, the measure used is solely that of raw political power.

**Protecting parents**

It is worth recalling here that there are political movements with significant degrees of influence – not least woke ones which regard tradition as the fruit of unjust hierarchies –who see parents as a hindrance to social progress. On the other hand, major business interests can be easily swayed – or bullied – into supporting progressive ideas which might lessen parental control on potential child consumers. Political movements see crèches, pre-schools and schools as valid targets to advance their agendas. Whereas they see parents as unwelcome carriers or defenders of tradition – which can often act as a dampener on new ideas, ensuring that the crazier ideas do not get a foothold in society.

Catholic schools of their nature recognise parents as primary educators, and see themselves *in loco parentis*. When true to their ethos, such schools are likely to be more intolerant of novelty posing in the guise of new learning. For example, the gender identity movement has much ideological nonsense associated with it, without mentioning the harmful psychological effects some of it can have on children's development over time. Educational ideas need to be grounded in reason, whereas most current woke thinking on gender and race has little or no intellectual basis, and is associated with poor, inadequate sociological research.

**Life through a secularist lens**

One such example is that of a private school in New York which in spring 2021 issued guidelines to students and parents encouraging them to alter their language in line with current gender-identity ideology, which included asking students to stop referring to their parents as 'mom' and 'dad' and to use terms such as 'grown-ups', 'folks' or 'family'. Some other recommended nomenclature in this guide included:

- Rather than 'assuming gender based on stereotypes' people should 'respectfully ask how they identify, establishing a culture of sharing affirming pronouns in class'.
- Instead of 'boys and girls', or 'ladies' or 'gentlemen', the terms 'people', 'folks', friends should be used.
- Rather than 'parents' say, 'grown-ups,' 'folks,' 'family,' 'and guardians.'
- Rather than say, 'husband, 'wife,' 'boyfriend,' 'girlfriend' say, 'spouse/partner/significant other.'
- Instead of asking, 'what religion are you?' ask 'are any religious/faith traditions important to you?'

The Irish response to such nonsense is generally that this cannot or will not happen here. But then it does, often sold in the fuzzy guise of making society more inclusive or compassionate in some way. There are organisations operating within Irish teacher unions who see life through the politicised lens of sexuality and who would prefer that gender neutral language was used in schools and that terms such as boy and girl be dispensed with. At a 2020 INTO conference, a spokesperson for one such organisation made little of the idea that parents might be consulted – in that case it was with regard to RSE programmes in schools. When confronted with such views, parents who wish to have their outlook of the natural family respected should find the protection they need in coherently Catholic school environments.

Catholic education is built on long-established principles, which if adhered to, protect young people, teachers and parents from experiencing political overreach into the system of education.

### *Endnotes*

**Keeping Woke thinking at a distance** – For the effect of woke thinking in elite US schools see for example *city-journal.org 'The misdirection of America's Elites'* by Bari Weiss, 9 March 2021.

For **Oregon Department of Education guidelines** see *https://content.govdelivery.com/accounts/ORED/bulletins/2bfbb9b?fbclid=IwAR3U8iS7fCD-g0NArQh74qlRa5IVFiTXoithZA89kMvmD0DETmzcV9DuQdg*

**According to one US Professor** – an Associate Dean at Arizona State University. See *Labor-Based Grading Contracts: Building Equity and Inclusion in the Compassionate Writing Classroom (Perspectives on Writing)* by Asao B Inoue (CSU Open Press, 2019).

**Such views are currently promoted in material appearing on the Teaching Council website** – see for example under Inclusion an article by Anastasia Liasidou, *'Inclusive education and critical pedagogy at the intersection of disability, race, gender and class,'* Journal for Critical Education Policy Studies 10.1 (2012), 168-184

For **guide issued by Grace School New York** see *GCS Inclusive Language Guide* on their website www.gcschool.org/programs/antiracism-equity-and-belonging.

**Protecting parents** – see Hilary Egan of the Irish National Teachers Organisation LGBT + in a video on Teaching Council website entitled '*Creating an LGBT+ inclusive primary school*'.

**2020 INTO conference** – statements made by Dr Elly Barnes, founder of Educate and Celebrate, speaking at an INTO conference in February 2020.

# SECTION 6
# Appreciating how Catholic education is different

One might have thought that in a freedom-loving society any well-established law-abiding group which clearly outlines its vision should be able to transmit that vision to others, and especially to those who wish to avail of it.

Yet the current secular vision of the state – which has no basis in the Irish Constitution – is to seek to improperly impose itself on Catholic schools.

Catholic educational institutions need to be more forthright in explaining their worldview, pointing out where the differences to the secular worldview lie. They also need to show how such Catholic differences can strengthen democracy, so that Catholic ideas and schools receive the widespread support from the general public that they deserve.

# Chapter 22
# Similar language, different identities

> **Key Takeaways**
>
> *At a superficial level there is little that distinguishes the mission statement of Educate Together and Catholic schools, other than that a Catholic might speak additionally of a learning environment inspired by the Gospels. Some of this apparent sameness is due to the ambiguity of language used.*
>
> *Catholic morality is anchored in objective truth, accessible by reason and knowable by reflecting on creation. The morality preferred by Educate Together does not generally commit to objective truth. It highlights personal autonomy, which is sometimes attained at the expense of the common good.*
>
> *A fully secular education, which denies that truth can be found in any religion, appears to be the preferred model for UN agencies.*

As an exercise in understanding 'characteristic spirit (or 'ethos') and its impact on the educational experience of young people it may prove helpful to compare and contrast the Catholic ethos with that of Educate Together schools and also with the type of secular education sought by Atheist Ireland.

Educate Together schools have a well-developed ethos for primary and secondary schools which is often termed multi-denominational. Their expressed vision is that all people would have access to inclusive education irrespective of belief system, race, ethnicity, class, culture, gender, language and ability. Educate Together's mission is to be an agent for change ensuring that parents have the choice of an education based on the inclusive intercultural values of respect for difference plus justice and equality for all. Using its own terminology, Educate Together schools are 'inclusive, democratic, co-educational, equality-based settings'. Although the term inclusive is undefined it is meant to include both a cultural and a religious object.

The vision, as outlined in the paragraph above, could equally be used to describe any Catholic school, but it would need to include in addition that the education takes place 'in a learning environment inspired by the life and teaching of Jesus Christ as seen in the Gospels.'

**Comparing mission statements**

Let us examine in a little more detail the four main elements highlighted in the Educate Together school mission.

*Equality-based education:* that is, all children have equal rights of access to the school, so that children of all social, cultural and religious backgrounds are equally respected.

There are varying approaches to the idea of access for a Catholic-based school. In the main Catholic schools do provide equality of access, although often preferring to accept families who are seeking a Catholic-identity school as opposed to families who might object to such an education. (Recent legislation has now removed the capacity of Catholic schools to choose Catholics over those with other religious beliefs where a school is oversubscribed, at the same time reinforcing the geographic nature of community over that of a religious-formed community). Catholic schools also claim to be equality-based. Both Catholic and Educate Together schools undertake to respect other cultures and religions. For an Educate Together model this might mean celebrating all religions equally, whereas for the Catholic model it would mean showing respect for the person's right to freedom of religion, while not celebrating their religious view as being as equally true as the Catholic faith. The Catholic model is committed to Catholicism as the one true faith, recognising that other religions have elements of truth, and fully respecting the rights of others to hold the beliefs of their religions as true.

*Co-educational*: An Educate Together school is co-educational and is committed to encouraging all children to explore their full range of abilities and opportunities. Boys and girls learn and socialize together in the school environment. The Educate Together claim – which other educationalists might dispute – is that this approach delivers the best educational and social development for children.

Traditionally, in Ireland, schools were mostly single-sex schools and this tradition still pertains in many Catholic schools today. So a Catholic ethos school might or might not be co-educational. There are conflicting views in educational literature on whether co-educational or single-sex education provide better academic or better all-round outcomes. At a minimum, given that both systems appear well matched, this then suggests that a mix of school types will best serve parental choice.

***Child-centred***: According to their literature, Educate Together schools are committed to active-learning techniques that encourage children to interact with their peers and teachers while they learn. Educate Together schools are focused on helping each individual child reach full academic and social potential.

All Catholic ethos schools would likely agree with the above and follow the modern educational dictum of putting the child at the centre of the learning experience. Catholic schools are committed to a holistic education.

***Democratically run:*** In Educate Together schools this is achieved with 'active participation by parents in the daily life of the school', whilst positively affirming the professional role of teachers.

Democratically-run schools are not the same as democratic schools. Democratic schools pursue democratic education, in which democracy is both a goal and a method of instruction. As one might imagine, such democratic schools would be viewed as highly experimental in nature and could never fit in with the top-down education model required by the Department of Education. On the other hand, democratically-run schools focus on school structure so that 'all voices are heard', and ultimate decisions are taken (at some level) on a majority basis.

There are very few democratic schools worldwide – simply because such institutions have not been shown to work. Nevertheless, emerging woke influences in education do promote more democratic methods of learning – for example, in the area of assessment – such as dis-empowering teachers, and pose a potential future threat to education systems.

Catholic schools would also claim to have democratic structures – with schools being under the control of Board of Managements, set up in line with the

1998 Education Act to represent the voice of teachers, parents and trustees in the overall management of the school. Schools will also normally have Parent Councils and Student Councils to represent their respective interests. Catholic schools explicitly recognise parents as the primary educators and that a Catholic school acts *in loco parentis*. By these means, parents' inalienable natural rights regarding the education of their child are additionally protected. Educate Together schools are not as forward as Catholic-ethos schools in acknowledging such parental rights. Such rights might come to the fore if a parent wished to withdraw their child from a particular class on grounds of conscience.

## Where the differences lie – anchoring truth and morality

Using the Educate Together descriptors above to make comparisons, this review of the mission and vision of Catholic and multi-denominational schools does not immediately reveal much by way of difference between school types. That is not surprising since the focus has mainly reflected school structures. A little more digging is required to explore what each school type understands by the language it uses, and to see how that difference impacts on the school curricula. Educate Together schools make no judgements about the value of any religion, thus implying that religions are all equal in value, whatever that value is taken to be. Likewise, such schools do not make any clear commitment to defining virtue or any specific values, in keeping with not being committed to any specific objective truth. Morality is similarly unanchored, since it is not possible to derive right and wrong from any objective source. Thus it becomes at best a vague unfocussed reflection of Christian values.

Insofar as Educate Together schools make objective moral claims – as for example they might do in opposing bullying – the grounding of these claims, when examined, is ultimately dependent on natural moral reasoning itself sourced in natural and, ultimately, eternal law. In order to anchor values for wider society, Educate Together schools appear to look to human rights treaties as the common ground on which people agree (and which ultimately – at least originally – reflect self-evident natural law truths).

In such an environment, moral decision-making will generally involve each individual doing what is right for the individual *me* – highlighting personal autonomy – and would look to unanchored or undefined ideas of justice, 'caring', 'equality' and stewardship of the environment. It is not clear to what extent the terms 'caring' and 'equality' would include placing personal responsibilities on the same level as personal rights or indeed whether these terms might even find room for the idea of self-sacrifice.

For Catholic-ethos schools there is a commitment to objective truth, based on the Christian understanding of God, which gives an anchor for right and wrong. The Catholic school focus is on encouraging a way of life which involves a commitment to virtue; to specific gospel values including moral decision-making in the context of an objective moral order; to human rights and justice, based on the innate dignity of all created persons, objective natural law and including social justice; and to stewardship of the environment as a duty to the Creator and to humankind. Thus the focus in Catholic schools is on instilling a firm foundation so that young people know the ground on which they stand – and on which they can naturally stay or depart as they grow to maturity – and which Catholic schools understand to be a true education in freedom.

Often the degree to which Educate Together schools mirror this commitment to objective truth will be the degree to which the specific Catholic understanding still holds sway in the wider culture. Catholic schools have, for example, clear principled grounds on which to resist gender ideology – i.e. to say that gender is not separable from biological sex. But should the wider culture claim otherwise, it seems more likely that Educate Together schools would follow that lead.

**Which morality can best contain individualism?**

To partially understand how secular and Christian morality can influence outcomes, consider the problem of toxic individualism which can be seen on both the left and right of the political spectrum. The emphasis on individualism has now devolved from an incomplete set of personal autonomy principles into an excuse for forsaking basic responsibilities such as, for example: not wanting the inconvenience of a family; abandonment of existing family responsibilities; financial greed; unfounded claims of victimhood; road rage; and more publicly aggressive real and online behaviours.

Christian morality tackles such toxic individualism head-on by highlighting the existence of right and wrong, by its focus on the common good of all and in its emphasis on the duty of charity. On the other hand, secular morality opens the door to such individualism by its materialist approach and by its overarching emphasis on personal autonomy. Once personal autonomy holds sway, the common good becomes a question of how can I achieve my claimed right while minimising the negative impact on others, rather than the common good of the whole of society. And so, for example, a claim of a right to die at the time of one's own choosing has little sympathy for how assisted suicide might impact significantly on the right to life of very many others.

**Are there differences in teaching and learning approaches?**

The pedagogies used in Catholic and Educate Together schools need not necessarily vary, but Catholic pedagogies are less open to political ideologies. With western society currently being threatened with the woke worldview the Catholic approach to education has some strong built-in protections. For example, Catholic pedagogy in encouraging us to learn from the past is less likely to be influenced by attempts to rewrite history under ideological duress as currently promoted by woke cultures. It is also more likely to affirm the traditional teacher-learner relationship over any democratic learning models which diminish the role of the teacher. It has a firm view on what human excellence is, by looking at the person of Christ. And it has rational ways of evaluating excellence, so that it will continue to assess it on the basis of competency. Catholic education understands the idea of forgiveness and so can promote reconciliation within society. Because it grounds morality in nature and reason it is less likely to allow indoctrination, such as that currently promoted by WHO in its sex education model. Because it is driven by a search for objective truth while affirming the beliefs of others, as well as everyone's capacity to find the truth, Catholic education will always promote dialogue as the path to peace – as opposed to routine exclusion, censoring or silencing of those in the public square.

**Where the differences lie – parents and teachers**

The expectation of teachers in an Educate Together school is that they be professional and objective. A Catholic school would express an additional expectation – that they be role models in the virtues that they articulate.

Parents in an Educate Together school are offered – for their children – an education based on the inclusive intercultural values of respect for difference and justice and equality for all. A Catholic school offers parents – for their children – access to an education based on a Christian vision of the world, which also includes justice, respect for difference and inclusiveness. Educate Together will additionally offer to facilitate specific education instruction in Religion – to take place after school hours. Unlike Catholic schools, it is not clear that Educate Together schools have a basis for acknowledging conscience rights of individual parents who might wish their children to opt out of aspects of the normal school-day curriculum.

**Some things look the same, yet are very different**

Overall, then, in describing Educate Together and Catholic schools much of the language used may be similar but the meanings underpinning the words will often be different. Each school type can confidently use terms like inclusive, democratic and enabling of children to achieve their full potential.

Aside from referring to its mission to prepare people for eternal life, what the Catholic school adds is a firm basis for truth, for objective right and wrong, and for morality, together with an understanding of freedom which highlights the importance of the common good and includes a more detailed specification of what being a caring, active and charitable member of society really means. Catholic schools, in specifically recognising parents as primary educators, are more likely in principle to respect conscience objections of parents.

This moral underpinning is of even greater import than simply teaching right and wrong. It also anchors the education system including its structures, curriculum and pedagogical methods, especially when these are under threat from wider ideologies – critical theory and woke thinking being modern examples of such dangers.

**Learning from each other**

While the purpose of this section has been to clearly delineate two educational visions, there will always be a blurring at the edges. Just as modern democracy has its roots in the Christian worldview so too does the multi-denominational sector draw on Christian principles. Some Educate Together schools will claim that their Ethics, even if these have been developed on a worldview different than Catholicism, are adequate to serve the needs of modern society. Many

Educate Together schools are valuably served by Catholic teachers and parents, which can help reduce the corrosive effect of secular doubt on individual, family and political life.

In a like manner many Catholic schools are served by non-practising teachers and parents who can help these schools purify their mission by demanding that they live up to the standards to which they attest.

It is the contention throughout this book that the principles of Catholic education are enduring and best serve young people in our society today, especially when similar values are lived and supported in the home. It is a very natural expectation that parents want to have schools which faithfully impart all that a Catholic school offers by way of faith, character education, values, methods of teaching and spirituality. It is also natural that others might not share this vision. What is not acceptable is that a secular worldview should seek by stealth to undercut parental rights in education.

**Secular education**

The Educate Together model is termed multi-denominational. Groups like Atheist Ireland would prefer to have a fully secular (or non-denominational) education system in which, as they see it, children are not treated differently on the basis of religion; where no religion has special privileges within the education system and where children are not required to be separated or excluded from selected classes.

In such a strictly secular model, religious symbols or practice would be generally restricted or prohibited in a school, and there might or might not be any explicit moral and ethical curriculum. This is because a secular school claims to be neutral on the question of religion – it makes no claims regarding the existence of God. Some secular schools would claim to teach children in an objective, critical, and pluralistic way about the different beliefs regarding God, leaving it up to parents and churches to teach specific religious beliefs outside of school hours.

This secular view is a relativistic pluralist view. It essentially presumes all religions are equally true or false. In doing this, it is actually denying that truth can be found in religion, while at the same time paradoxically proposing the study of many of them. The logic is that beliefs must be respected, or accommodated but not really be taken seriously. By direct contrast, an inclusive Catholic school brings everyone of religious and non-religious backgrounds together; it proposes a specific worldview and shows how any worldview can be evaluated in a genuine desire that all seek to obtain objective truth. In so doing, it opens doors of intellectual exploration in that search for truth while equipping students with the tools they need to interpret the world.

Viewed from the Catholic-ethos perspective a fully secular school might not be seen to be very much different in its general educational approach than that of an Educate Together school, aside from Religion or Ethics modules in the curriculum of the latter. However, insofar as spirituality or morality are integrated into anything in the curriculum, Educate Together schools are not acceptable to secularists.

## The international political view

Having claimed all the neutral ground to themselves, secularists insist that all schools should be state-funded secular schools. Many would rightly dispute such claims. Should one view atheism as a belief system – *as in effect it is* since it does have a set of core beliefs – then the ludicrous nature of this claim by a miniscule section of the population is laid bare.

The call for secular education is not just being made by a small number of secularists or atheists in Ireland. In spite of UN human rights affirming school choice, the UN Human Rights Committee in 2016 recommended that Irish students have access to secular education and it encouraged the phasing out of religious integrated curricula in the majority of schools.

The UN Universal Declaration on Human Rights makes a clear statement regarding parents' rights in education in Article 26. Having affirmed the right of everyone to education it states that 'Parents have a prior right to choose the kind of education that shall be given to their children' (point 3). Article 18.4 of the International Covenant on Civil and Political Rights concurs:

> The State Parties to the present Covenant undertake to have respect for the liberty of parents, and, when applicable, legal guardians to ensure the religious and moral education of their children in conformity with their own convictions.

Nonetheless, UN Committees, which unfortunately often represent an ideologically-driven worldview, have a distinct preference for secularist or non-denominational schooling. Even if not directly mandating secular schools, they recommend programmes which derive from secularist thinking and express a strong desire for the removal of religious influence and religious values from schools.

For example the UN Committee on the Convention for the Elimination of All Forms of Discrimination against Women (CEDAW) proposed in 2017 that the Irish State adopt a sex-education model free from moral influences. They asked that Ireland

> Integrate compulsory and standardised age-appropriate education on sexual and reproductive health and rights into school curricula, including comprehensive sex education for adolescent girls and boys covering responsible sexual behaviours and focused on preventing early pregnancies; and ensure that it is scientifically objective and its delivery by schools is closely monitored and evaluated.

That Committee also expressed concern at 'reports of stereotypes and sexism in the field of education' and at

> the narrow approach towards the provision of sexuality education due to the fact that the content of the Relationship and Sexuality Education (RSE) curriculum is left to institutions to deliver it according to the schools ethos and values and as a result it is often taught together with biology and religious courses.

Among negative issues highlighted in 2016 by the UN Committee on the Rights of the Child's (UNCRC) Report on Ireland were

> The lack of non-denominational schools for children to attend and the number of schools that continue 'to practice discriminatory admissions policies on the basis of the child's religion.'

and

> The lack of available abortion in Ireland and 'the severe lack of access to

sexual and reproductive health education and emergency contraception for adolescents.'

**Looking to the future on offer**

The ideology of secularism, sold under the guise of neutrality, if successful in its ambition, would ultimately result in the removal of religion as a vital cultural and intellectual dimension of education. Catholic educators thus need to equip themselves well in fighting their corner for Catholic education.

Models of schooling which ignore or deny God's existence leave modern reason only with 'facts' to work with – together with the recent additional handicap of being unable to properly weigh what are presented as facts from real facts, to distinguish misinformation from information. Such limited 'reason', without any understanding of our nature, can only suggest that right and wrong for the individual will depend on the situation in the here and now. Schooling which is based on such principles may be akin to the blind leading the blind. And without objective morality, even their pedagogy becomes vulnerable to the prevailing ideological winds.

A clear realism is promoted in Catholic-Christian schools and has a pedagogy to accompany it. God exists, as does objective truth. There is a right and wrong. Reason is important but Catholics also realise that reason alone is insufficient to establish any morality. Reason additionally needs to remember that it is anchored in our given nature as creatures. The world is not primarily about the individual, about 'me', but is fully about 'me with others', which then places my responsibilities to others on a par with my rights. Charity has a meaning. Bearing in mind all these realities, truly Catholic schools educate the whole person in an integral way for freedom.

The words of the psalmist capture the mind of a Christian educator with regard to God: 'A lamp for my feet and a light for my path.' Educators need to hold on firmly to that lamp. A good step would be for Catholic schools to improve in their efforts to be Catholic.

## Endnotes

**respecting the rights of others to hold the beliefs of their religions as true:** The Declaration of the Second Vatican Council (1965) on the *Relation of the Church to non-Christian religions (Nostra Aetate)*, 2 states: 'Likewise, other religions found everywhere try to counter the restlessness of the human heart, each in its own manner, by proposing "ways," comprising teachings, rules of life, and sacred rites. The Catholic Church rejects nothing that is true and holy in these religions. She regards with sincere reverence those ways of conduct and of life, those precepts and teachings which, though differing in many aspects from the ones she holds and sets forth, nonetheless often reflect a ray of that Truth which enlightens all men. Indeed, she proclaims, and ever must proclaim Christ "the way, the truth, and the life" (John 14:6), in whom men may find the fullness of religious life, in whom God has reconciled all things to Himself.

The Church, therefore, exhorts her sons, that through dialogue and collaboration with the followers of other religions, carried out with prudence and love and in witness to the Christian faith and life, they recognize, preserve and promote the good things, spiritual and moral, as well as the socio-cultural values found among these men.'

# Chapter 23
# Facing up to the political landscape

> **Key Takeaways**
>
> *Catholics rightly oppose secular education because it refuses to address the most fundamental reality of life, i.e. God's existence and all that flows from it. The purely functional nature of secular education is not holistic.*
>
> *In recent years, state agencies have sided with the secular worldview.*
>
> *There are no pressing reasons why a national curriculum cannot respect a range of ethos options and thus the freedom for Catholics in education.*
>
> *There are common-sense ways to advance the divestment of Catholic primary schools. Respecting diversity and personal freedoms are not a problem for denominational schools.*
>
> *Catholic schools need to have more confidence in the quality of the product they have to offer to students, parents and democratic society, while constantly seeking to improve it.*

**Intolerance in the media**

The Irish state is as open to international political pressures as any other state. International agencies, influenced primarily by modern Western culture, take a predominantly secularist view of the world. This may be understandable and might even be acceptable if these did not seek to impose their worldview with true zeal. In the Western world it is often Catholic voices who resist such secular fundamentalism, standing up for personal freedoms to live lives in line with God's vision for his creation. Schools, working with families, are important places where those freedom values can be transmitted.

Unfortunately, due to similar secularist ideologies holding a prominent place in Irish media, it is seldom that voices contrary to the secular worldview are heard. For example, the general public will have heard about President Biden's professed Catholicism but almost nothing has been reported on the religious reaction against his pro-abortion stances on coming into office. Most have witnessed liberal tolerance of inappropriate censorship by the social media tech giants but hear no critique of this or of Eastern European religiously-inspired attempts to ensure freedom of expression. Many have seen Poland criticised for planning to withdraw from a UN treaty but few have heard that Poland seeks to do so to avoid enforced gender-identity measures. Opposition in Ireland to proposed RSE programmes has been explained by our media in terms of malicious scaremongering and misinformation and not what actually inspires that opposition – a deep, well-placed suspicion of the imposition of a secular belief system. As pointed out earlier, elements in our media are no strangers to intolerant anti-Catholic sentiment. As long as this informs our media discourse it will continue to be difficult to have proper public debate in Ireland.

**The State is taking sides**

There is a broad range of genuinely different opinions on how to manage our educational system. Unfortunately, the cultivated narrative has tended to run along anti-Catholic lines. Simply put, the narrative maintains that our education system is controlled by the Catholic Church; it is discriminatory; as many schools as possible should be handed over by the Church, or taken from them, and all remaining Catholic schools should be forced to adopt a 'pluralist' , that is, secular, ethos.

The clearest opposing view to Catholic education requests that all education be secular as this means, as they see it, all children will experience equal dignity and equal respect for their human rights. This view sees denominational education as effectively sectarian in nature and therefore incompatible with equal treatment.

Those defending Catholic schools or faith-based approaches to education are not looking for exclusivity – far from it. Yet the opposition voices that receive the greatest media amplification want exclusivity in line with the above narrative – that is, a purely secular school system. Why is this? What actually has secular education going for it? Even its very capacity to be manipulated by trending political ideologies should be a warning of its inherent inadequacies. It may be that those seeking change have a greater commitment towards achieving their vision than those defending faith-based education. It may be that a lack of ability to publicly articulate what it means to be faith-based has led to a wider lack of appreciation of the underlying values. It may also relate to past failures or to an unjust silencing of Catholic voices. Whatever the reason, Catholic schools need to be more vocal about what they regard as important to them or they may be faced with finding out what will be imposed on them.

The Catholic argument is simple. For it, secular education is not holistic education because it refuses to address the most fundamental reality of our existence – God's existence – and all that stems from it: the eternal destiny and hence dignity of the human person, the importance of truth, distinguishing right from wrong, responsibilities deriving from our sociability, and the meaning of charity. Catholics wish their children to be educated in Catholic schools, and that these schools be allowed to be properly Catholic, and not be treated as second-class through improper use of any state-funding mechanisms.

This is not special pleading but a respect for the fundamental freedoms of Catholic citizens. It could also be categorised as a right to have one's choice respected. Education is primarily the responsibility of parents, not the state. School systems or educational programmes should not undermine or threaten parents' abilities to raise their children in line with their beliefs and values. As argued clearly in '*To Whom Do Children Belong*' robust parental rights best serve parents, children and society as a whole.

The State would appear to be taking sides, sometimes surreptitiously. For example, the language used by the NCCA in developing ERB & Ethics programmes makes it sound that a world that does not acknowledge God's existence is no different than one which does. Less hidden was the earlier discussed parliamentary attempt to remove the right to subject any proposed RSE programme to standard school-ethos scrutiny. The 1998 Education Act shows respect for management authorities to implement their ethos fully. Therefore schools should not be afraid nor be slow to stand in the shade of this Act while delivering on their Catholic mandate.

**Responding to pressure**

Should state authorities seeks to exercise further muscle through a misuse of the public purse to bring about unwanted change in Catholic schooling, then

Catholics need to remember that it is their money that forms a substantial part of that public purse. This is fundamentally an issue of parental choice exercised in conjunction with schools who are providing the Catholic education these parents desire. If the State cannot see its way to allow Catholic schools to be Catholic, and by extension allow other schools maintain their ethos, then it would make more democratic sense for the State to substantially withdraw from education and develop a voucher system so that taxpayers could use their educational taxes to support the alternatives they prefer.

There are all sorts of financial solutions which can end up in the same place, that is, respecting the right of Catholic schools to be Catholic (and, by inference, other schools to uphold their own characteristic spirit). Catholic schools would be betraying their identity and their parent and student bodies, and indeed the principles of freedom which impact on other educational models, if they were to tolerate discrimination of any kind.

**Recognising diversity**

The proposed new primary school curriculum being developed by the NCCA and the outlines available to date of a proposed RSE programme clearly indicate an inability to provide for curricular diversity, due to strong secular influences. Such attempts to enforce conformism are nothing new. No sooner had the new Junior Cycle programme been liberated from compulsory subjects and schools granted more autonomy for their curriculum than these new-found freedoms were rolled back.

There are no pressing academic reasons why a national curriculum cannot allow for a range of ethos options, one of which is acceptable to Catholic or other religious ethos groups, and another which is acceptable to a multi-denominational or even to a purely secular sector. The notion that a one-size-fits-all curriculum is satisfactory or even necessary for a modern, diverse democratic society is illogical.

This argument should not be presented as a plea for special treatment for Catholic schools. Rather it is a call that education be properly freed from political influence, in this case the baneful influence of political secular thinking. Catholic freedom in education is a freedom for all in education.

## Divestment of patronage of primary schools

In 2012, The Forum for Patronage and Pluralism recommended divestment of patronage of a substantial number of primary schools from the Catholic Church, in order to meet the demand for secular education. The report suggested that the move towards more non-religious control of schools should happen in a phased manner. Only a very small number of schools have changed patronage since then, although a more significant number of new non-religious schools have opened. Currently, almost 90% of primary schools are under Catholic patronage in a country where 78% identify as Catholic, and where the non-religious population has grown by 70% over six years. So it would certainly seem there is a prima facie case for more divestment.

There are those, not surprisingly, who are quick to blame the Church for the slow pace of change, yet there are not many management boards of existing schools lining up seeking to be divested. It may simply be that when the issue arises of a school continuing to be Catholic or not, there may be more loyalty to Catholic education than to unclear, alternative secular or multidenominational models.

The divestment programme is primarily an issue for the State to resolve. It must ensure that in each case where it occurs it is made easy for parents who express opposition to move their children to other schools. Schools will also need to have the flexibility to adjust to divestment, for example, by being able to redeploy teachers between schools, or being able to address transport issues arising for children affected by redeployment. Financial compensation issues for parishes may need some consideration.

The Catholic Church should also be keen to make it happen, so as to facilitate the rights of non-Catholics, or of those not wishing to avail of Catholic education. There may now be a good case for some parishes to seek to organise sacramental preparation on a parish basis rather than a school basis, especially if there is a significant minority of students not involved. Not only will this take pressure off the school curriculum in some cases, but it will allow parishes to form more natural bonds with young Catholic families. It may also make it easier for Catholic school management to maintain a Catholic ethos if there are not significant groups of unhappy parents feeling that their educational rights are in some way being undermined.

## Facing up to the political landscape

There are clear downsides in taking sacramental preparation out of Catholic primary schools, as to some degree it can undermine the collaboration envisaged between the home, school and parish. It will require more well-educated lay catechists, as there are insufficient priests available. Lessening the catechetical involvement of schools may also strengthen the hand of those wishing to impose the secular ERB and Ethics in all schools.

That said, should the divestment issue be left unresolved, then most new schools will end up by default being allotted to non-religious patrons in an attempt to correct the national imbalance, possibly leaving many new housing areas without a Catholic-ethos school.

The corollary to an efficient divestment process should be a reinforcing of the right of remaining Catholic schools to live by their Catholic characteristic spirit and for the State to resist international secularisation forces requiring a secular school system in Ireland.

Much store is placed by those seeking divestment in Article 2 of Protocol 1 to the European Convention on Human Rights which says:

> In the exercise of any functions which it assumes in relation to education and to teaching, the State shall respect the right of parents to ensure such education and teaching in conformity with their own religious and philosophical convictions.

This is also an article which Catholic schools can lean on to protect the characteristic spirit of their own schools. Despite claims to the contrary, this article does not impose a positive obligation for States to create a public education system that is secular.

As more divestment takes place there is obviously a clear onus on the State to support Catholic schools seeking to retain their own identity. At present, as can be seen from creeping secularisation – witness the examples outlined in Section Five – there would not seem to be any clear will within the political establishment to do that.

## Conscience opt outs

It makes sense that, within reason, school staff and students should not be obliged to act against their conscience, and that Catholic schools in particular be cognisant of that. Thus a teacher who is not practising his or her Catholic faith, or who has another religious allegiance or none, might not wish to prepare a class for Confirmation, or supervise them while attending a liturgical act. A non-Catholic parent might not wish their child to attend religious education in a Catholic school. A parent might wish their child to opt out of an RSE class on the basis of the programme content.

In all such circumstances common sense and a respect for personal freedoms must prevail. If a staff member or teacher is working in a school with a clear ethos then they normally would be expected to support that ethos or, at a minimum, not seek to undermine it. In that case then, a Catholic school would do its best to honour the request of the teacher, yet it might need to insist – because it has no choice – than this teacher carry out the undesired supervision work. A teacher cannot reasonably expect a vindication of opt-out rights which has the effect of nullifying a central commitment of a school to its families.

In a similar fashion, students who attend a particular ethos school must normally expect that the school will make certain demands of them, without impinging on their natural freedoms. If a student attends a multi-denominational school it would normally be unreasonable to expect that the student would receive a Catholic Religious Education programme within the school day. A Muslim child at a Catholic school should not be required to attend Religious Education against parental wishes, unless there really are no alternative supervision possibilities available – and in such cases the attendance should be merely passive.

From time to time, media stories suggest that Catholic schools are not inclusive, yet the Department of Education Inspector reports found an 'overwhelming majority of parents and students find their schools to be well-managed and welcoming'. Whatever the practicalities that prevail in any individual school, these should always seek to uphold conscience rights of students and staff.

The school system in Ireland has much to recommend it, not least the quality and vitality of the Catholic sector. For that to continue, Catholic schools may need to show more confidence in the product they are delivering while, like a good supplier, constantly upgrade the quality of merchandise on offer. Apart from the personal benefits accruing to all students concerned, Catholic education has an important role to play in helping society address the storms currently enveloping western democracy. Secularism is undermining democracy's foundations. To save democracy will require young people fully educated within the Catholic tradition who can revitalise the threatened freedoms that currently underpin democracy.

This book asks 'Our school is Catholic – so what?' Well, appreciate what being Catholic means; don't be slow to uphold or promote the brand; strive to maintain the vibrancy that comes from presenting a coherent Catholic outlook to students; and in doing all this, the fundamental democratic freedoms you value for society are more likely to prevail.

### Endnotes

**2020 Programme for Government** – see *Our Shared Future* (Government Publications 2020)

**A voucher system**. Voucher systems in education can take many forms depending on the purpose. Essentially these exist to enable parents to enrol a child in the school of their choice with the state paying via a voucher to the school. For details on existing systems see *School Choice and School Vouchers: An OECD perspective* (OECD 2017). A new radical education savings account (i.e. voucher) system has recently been adopted in West Virginia (USA). Families can receive an annual education voucher totalling 100% of what the state would have spent on a child's education in a public school and instead of attending the local school this money can be spent on online learning, private school tuition, private tutoring and other education services.

**To whom do children belong:** 'what we really mean is – who has primary responsibility for children and decision-making power over them?' The author grounds her argument for parent rights on the special obligations inherent in the parent-child relationship. See *To Whom Do Children Belong* by Melissa Moschella (Cambridge University Press 2016).

**'find their schools to be well-managed and welcoming'** – the claim is made that an ESRI report and DES Inspectorate reports support this view. See Ferdia Kelly of the Catholic School Partnership quoted in in Irish Times article *Forced into Faith*, 8 May 2017

# Appendix 1
# Implementing Character Education in schools

**What is character education?**

A person of character is one who integrates the key traits or good habits that one would wish to have – habits, for example, such as sound judgement, a sense of responsibility, courage, self-mastery, and generosity. Such good dispositions or habits enable young people to flourish intellectually, personally and socially, thus making it easier for them to choose the good, even when it is difficult.

Character education then is the process involved in helping young people acquire these key traits, virtues or good habits. It is a deliberate effort to help people understand, care about, and act to do the good thing – that is to know, love and do the good. And the content of character education is the activity of helping them acquire these key traits, virtues or good habits.

Thus character education cannot be reduced to delivering a short course, a few lessons, a wall-poster or notice-board announcements. It should rather be a full and integral part of school life. Schools know they are succeeding in this work when a student can speak as freely about improvement in his or her personal virtue as he or she can speak about improvement in mathematical skills or in reading or research skills.

All Catholic schools should aspire to be character education schools. The initial effort required may be substantial but the rewards can be considerable for the school, its students and their parents.

**The rewards**

The primary benefits are reaped by the student. Ultimately, educators seek to prepare the young person for a successful and happy life. Freedom is an important part of that, and virtues or good habits are necessary if the student is to control his or her passions and emotions and to live freely. It is obvious that a person dominated by a passion such as envy or greed or anger has only a limited freedom, just as a person who hasn't learn to play the piano while young is not 'free', that is, unable, to give a public concert.

For good or ill, Irish society has now become a more non-directive society, leaving people to make their own decisions, even with friends displaying a reluctance to interfere or to suggest a more moral direction. A young person trained in virtue has many worthwhile building blocks in place to help him or her to survive in such a climate and is better placed to evaluate the right thing to do in a particular circumstance.

Developing habits such as patience, serenity and resilience help people face up to the difficulties in life, which can be more marked in circumstances of hardship or austerity. Good habits such as diligence, sincerity, personal accountability, courage and perseverance enable people to develop better personal relationships and to work better.

There are also enormous benefits redounding to the school from character education. Any educational institution actively promoting virtue will be a much calmer and respect-filled environment, which is then an enjoyable place for all students and teachers to work. Also, many virtues have an impact on academic performance: virtues such as industriousness, diligence and patience enable young people to be better persons and better students.

**An area for a home-school partnership**

Character education is part of the primary job of parents. Yet, as parents get caught up more and more in workplace demands, they often require additional help from schools. In such circumstances the school can take a stronger leadership role in this vital education task of forming character. And whereas younger children may prove a more fertile furrow, the task reaches its maximum effectiveness if schools and parents can continue united in the character-education task right through adolescence and indeed through all of secondary school.

For maximum effectiveness:

- The school (and also the family) need to work consistently at character education. (Just as a student's reading capabilities can be best developed by a plan which operates consistently in school and at home, so too with character development.)

- The school and family reinforce each other by singing from the same hymn-sheet. A consistency of effort and a unity of thought is thereby achieved. (This means a lot of additional work will be required by schools to firstly educate parents in what their joint objectives should be and secondly in the methods to be used in achieving these.)

- Parents need to be open to what the school has to say and what it does. Because judgments are being made which entail some subjective dimensions, schools will be slow to make them if they sense that parents will be uncooperative.

- Character education is always work in progress – there are no short cuts. Confidence in its longer-term effectiveness, as well as patience, perseverance and optimism will all be required in the face of natural adolescent setbacks in secondary school.

The National Centre for Educational Statistics in the US surveyed 25,000 students and came to the conclusion (which may perhaps be obvious to Irish parents and teachers) that parental involvement in school correlates with higher grade-point averages (that is, exam results). There is no reason to suppose that active parental involvement will not also bear significant character benefits for students.

**A clear need for society**

Any overworked educator with limited experience of character education will balk at the idea of the additional workload a school could bring upon itself. Yet, if Catholic schools are to honour their commitment to an integral education so that young people can make a difference in their societies, then it is hard to see how they can do otherwise.

A practical 'business case' can easily be made for character education. More and more employers are dissatisfied with the basic human formation of young people emerging from the third-level system. They may know their science or accountancy but they are often poor in team work and social skills, often lacking in dress sense, manners and personal respect.

Also, it is widely understood that over 30% of people in leadership positions have behavioural issues which inhibit their effectiveness: e.g. they may be histrionic, or poor listeners, disorganised, cynical, asocial, obsessive, or may not communicate effectively with their employees.

These unhelpful traits, if directly challenged through a character education programme, might not be so prevalent in our adult society.

It may be that for too long Irish second-level schools have associated character education primarily or solely with sport and that the character requirements of elite sports was the sum total of what character education was about. Promoting strong team loyalty may help prepare young people for the battlefield but it can also lead to closed groups, an old-school-tie exclusivity, and to cover-ups when things go wrong. Aggression and self-belief which may be appropriate for the playing field will not help prepare future parents in the virtues of gentleness, humility and self-sacrifice which will be needed in the home. It may not be accidental in Irish society that heavy drinking and sport are linked, both being associated with a he-man macho culture. It is not that sporting virtues should not be taught, but that there is much, much more to character education – and it is often overlooked.

At a minimum, if young people learn the tools of self-evaluation as provided through character education, then they are more likely to apply them: the message of the Oracle 'know thyself' remains a perennial challenge.

**A true Christian endeavour**

A key word in character education is that of improvement. Some virtues are much harder to acquire than others. There can also be a genetic component associated with some virtues, thus making it more difficult for certain individuals to make progress. Temperament or personality types also play a part. Students with certain learning difficulties may show a marked inability to progress, or occasionally even become obsessive about improvement.

Nonetheless, for each virtue there is a standard which can be set for any group, against which one person may achieve more than another. Young people naturally strive for improvement and have a desire to learn. Many indeed struggle to overcome failure or obstacles, so that the educator's role is to set realistic standards and goals, provide encouragement, and help the young person realise that success may be achievable only in very small steps, and that growing in virtue is one area where the learning can be truly lifelong. While members of a group can encourage each other, especially when younger, the only real competition should be each person against themselves. Inappropriate rewards for children in character education can provide unsuitable motivation, leading them to practice virtue primarily for reward and thus defeating the overall purpose.

Character education mirrors a Christian worldview. It connotes a recognition that there is no Utopia and that part of life is striving to be better. It also acknowledges that there is a right and wrong way to behave, that there is a good and a better, and that we benefit as individuals and as a society in striving for the better. When character education focuses on the social virtues it can be a reminder of the importance of other persons and acts as an antidote to the self-centred individualism of other worldviews.

The impact of the personal example of educators cannot be underestimated. An educator who models a virtue, particularly in dealing with adolescents, is more likely to be persuasive, given the heightened sense of justice among teenagers. Thus, for example, for a parent to be able to say to a child that members of this family behave in a certain way and not in another can be a powerful persuasive educational tool.

Ultimately, personal influence is the best educator. Thus, this needs to be considered in larger schools where educational staff can sometimes be too distant from students to be persuasive. Unfortunately nowadays a drive for wider subject choice creates a pressure for schools to be ever-increasing in size, often with negative implications for the school's character-education role.

Should a school need to constantly expand, it should also seek to ensure that the valuable human relationships between teacher and student are not undermined. This can be done by placing an upper limit on the number of students that individual teachers are required to educate. It is worth considering the outcome of research on the cognitive limit for the number of persons with whom one can maintain stable social relationships. The Dunbar number was proposed by a British anthropologist in the 1990's based on a correlation between primate brain size and average social group.

Dunbar proposed that humans can maintain 150 stable relationships, that is, relationships in which an individual knows who each person is and how each person relates to the other person. Even the existence of such a number should be an encouragement to schools to form appropriate-size education 'pods' so that teachers can know their students better and continue to have more human engagements with them.

In ideal circumstances, students seek to improve behaviour and attitudes; teachers, especially year-heads, encourage improvement in selected areas; students are encouraged to examine themselves on their own progress; while teachers and parents work together to seek improvement from the students. In this manner, the school acts like a wider family contributing to the transformative nature of any character education programme.

**Learning from character education in the home**

Character education is most effective when home and school are working together. A school's approach should seek to mirror that of the ideal home.

In promoting character education in the home, there are some practical reminders worth highlighting:

- Character education is best achieved through modelling good behaviour and through constant, non-confrontational instruction.

- Parents (as a couple or in groups) should review family living from time to time to ensure that the environment is conducive to the expectations they have for their children. This includes considering the organised times which the family spends together, meal-times and procedures, shared religious practice, managing friends and house visitors, what are and what are not family customs.

- Parents need to be alert to and aware of what is being done in the school by way of character education and back this up in an appropriate manner at home.

- Parents need to be aware of the strong influences on their children and speak regularly about these, especially as their children grow older. Children, while they outwardly react against boundaries, also inwardly appreciate them as it helps them to structure their behaviours. Good parents don't just simply say 'I trust my child', but rather 'I trust you, but I don't always trust your judgement.' Children are surrounded by strong influences, including easily accessible addictive possibilities, and by a peer group which may expect that loyalty to them be stronger than loyalty to one's family.

- Parents need to be alert to wider societal influences though internet, social media, television and phone use. Ever-present threats include cyber-bullying, pornography and addictive behaviours – some of which can be highly destructive of young people's lives and so should be an ever-present consideration for parents. Constant surveillance is part of the responsibility of parents since they may often be the sole line of defence available to their son or daughter. It is not a lack of trust in the young person, but an acknowledgement that their judgment is not sufficiently mature. If parents have been educating in character from an early age, then this alertness is second nature, and is also expected by the young person, even if it is not appropriately acknowledged.

- No matter what other pressures parents may be experiencing, they should always be talking with their children, especially during teenage years and as they approach adulthood. Parents should be firm – and fair – in laying down boundaries, being constant in enforcing them, and explaining them to the degree that is appropriate. Well-chosen boundaries provide security for young people.

Teachers, year-heads or guidance counsellors in a school setting would do well to review their roles as character educators in the light of the above good family practice.

**Character education in the school**

Similar to parents in a family, a school that is committed to character development stands for good character traits. The school

- defines them in terms of practical behaviours that can be observed in the day-to-day life of the school;

- realises that struggling to grow in virtue can be a strong unifying factor in any school (and across all cultural and religious beliefs);

- seeks that all staff model these virtues;

- allows opportunities in the curriculum and in extra-curricular settings to study and discuss them (for example, through the Wellbeing syllabus, but not exclusively so);

- uses them as the basis of personal relationships within the school;

- celebrates their visibility in the school and in the community;

- seeks to help all school members be accountable to standards of conduct consistent with these virtues.

Key virtues are then treated as a matter of obligation, as having a claim on the conscience of the individual and community. Character education in the school asserts that the validity of these virtues, and the responsibility on all to uphold them. The school proudly does so because such virtues affirm human dignity, promote the development and welfare of the individual person, and serve the common good.

There is an educational viewpoint which says that simply getting young people to do what they're told is character education. This idea often leads to an imposed set of rules and a system of rewards and punishments that produce temporary and limited behavioural changes, but they do little or nothing to affect the underlying character of young people. A character education school aims to develop independent thinkers who are committed to moral principles in their lives, and who are likely to do the right thing even under challenging circumstances. This requires a somewhat different approach than seeing personal behaviour distilled down to rules.

**Character education: the whole school approach**

The declared aim is to help students to be the best person they can be, using the opportunities provided in the school such as study, work, general behaviour, interaction with others, school responsibilities, occasions for

## Appendix 1

leadership, and extracurricular activity to help promote virtue. The value of a whole-school approach is lauded in relation to academic development. So it also is with character education. Schools are now familiar with examining how literacy or numeracy is progressed on a whole school basis – and similar exercises can be conducted around character education.

The following points should provide guidance to schools on integrating character education into every aspect of school life:

- A school should review which virtues or good character traits it wishes to promote at any given time, while also acknowledging what the key ones are.

- All school structures, procedures and events should show commitment to virtues. In exhorting students (through website, social media, contacts with parents, assembly, notice-boards, posters, or by teachers or other school staff) the school points out what good character traits it requires from its students. The various branches of the school: administration, management, teaching staff, caretaking staff should all seek to apply the same standards of good behaviour, explaining the standards expected and where necessary using appropriately staged sanctions in order to elicit improvement.

- The above presupposes that all school staff understand the need to model the virtues they expect young people to live.

- The school should promote ideas of hard work and study – these are key character shaping components, and the importance of related academic virtues as lifelong virtues should not be underestimated. Study is a key activity of every student, including during the holiday periods. Studiousness is an important means of developing personality, and in stimulating many capacities and human values, such as: constancy; silence; concentration; order; punctuality; completing tasks; a desire to overcome difficulties; and developing good work habits for the future.

- In the school's approach to academics, students should be encouraged to take responsibility for each other, emphasizing cooperation and collaboration and not just competition.

- All subjects on the curriculum should be examined to see where these can highlight character education. All curriculum areas dealing with Wellbeing should be structured around character education. The Physical Education syllabus and extra-curricular sport activities can be reviewed in the light of character-education. Unstructured play has an important place in developing good socialisation skills, learning to set goals, appreciating rules and realizing the importance of rest.

- Virtues such as perseverance, respect, industriousness and honesty can be part of everyday lessons. Schools should present role models to young people for consideration when they address character issues in the classroom.

- In order to form the moral understanding of young people, teachers can use the curriculum to present examples of what constitutes good or bad behaviour or where virtue is shown (e.g. the king who lacked self-discipline or the politician who displayed fortitude). The Relationship and Sexuality Education programme should extensively highlight the importance of human virtues such as charity, fortitude, chastity, self-control, good judgement and generosity in managing personal relationships.

- The school's behaviour code inside and outside of the classroom can be expressed in terms of virtue. A school's discipline procedures should strongly reflect a commitment to character formation. A key word for all this is 'improvement'. Students should seek to improve their behaviour and attitude; teachers and year heads should encourage improvement in selected areas and speak about the virtues. Teachers and parents should be encouraged to seek improvement from the students, and to get students to examine themselves with regard to improvement in virtue.

- Discipline and classroom management should concentrate on problem-solving and self-improvement rather than on rewards and punishments (but not to the exclusion of these standard elements of school life). The discipline system should aim to encourage freedom and personal responsibility. It should help people take responsibility for their actions and aim at self-improvement.

- Students need to be helped to have a sense of ownership for their school and its ethos as well as to be constantly reflecting on living out the virtues and on desires for improvement. Helping young people face up to responsibilities advances their personal maturity. Personal appraisal in virtue development should be part of the educational goals of a character-education school.

- Year heads and guidance supports within the school play an important role in promoting character building through group discussion, the organisation of extra-curricular activities which include character goals, the student's school Journal and meetings with parents.

- All students, including those exhibiting troublesome behaviour should be helped to take responsibilities within the school, however small. Leadership as a practical concept should be encouraged through school activities and in school assemblies.

- Families should be encouraged to work together and with the school in developing character education.

- The school needs to continually review relationships across the school: between and among students, staff, parents and the wider community. Such reviews need to consider how teachers are role models for the students; the quality of teacher-student interactions; whether the student body realises that everything about it, and about individual students matters to the school; how students are helped to respect each other's sameness yet difference; ensuring students on school trips are sensitive to the school's reputation; seeking to create a palpable family atmosphere of trust within the school; developing the school as a caring community through the promotion of social or service projects; promoting a fraternal sense among students in helping each other to work and in their specific studies; helping students appreciate their families more; involving families more in the school, especially in the character education effort.

- School events are important occasions for families to get know each other. This in turn helps them supervise and become more involved in the social interactions of their children.

**The school helps the home**

The more the school and home work together on character education the more that will be achieved. For this to happen:

- Both parents and school should use the student's school diary effectively as a transparent tool of communication.

- Parents need to converse more with their children. Parents who are actively involved in their school know more about it and often have more matters to discuss with their children.

- Parents need to converse more with each other, formally and informally, with a view to assisting in the management of their children's social lives and freedom.

- Parent social events in the school or in the local parish create the space to meet others and to share experiences, and thus are well worth the time invested.

- Subject teachers can be a very reliable source of information on a student's attitude to work and to others: for that reason parent-teacher meetings serve an important character education function.

**Does character education work?**

In short, yes. Character education schools exist and thrive, because any educational institution with an ethos which can be boiled down to a day-to-day lived experience will be successful.

In any school there are always things which can be done better. What a school says and does may not always tally; it may not be the experience of every individual student. Not everyone may sing the same tune all the time. But if there is a high degree of harmony between what a school says and what it does; between how it should do it and how it actually does it; and, in general, if the staff in the school work in close harmony with the school's overall aims and objectives, then the benefit to students and staff will be tangible and transformative.

In the context of Catholic schools in particular, character education provides a good unifying theme and properly helps broaden a person's understanding of religion beyond the confines of prayer.

In such a school, core Christian virtues can be treated as non-negotiable, as having a claim on the conscience of every individual and community.

# Appendix 1

Character education asserts the validity of these virtues, and the responsibility to uphold them, derived from the fact that such virtues affirm our human dignity, promote the development and welfare of the individual person, and serve the common good.

In an efficiently functioning character-education school, the return on the effort involved will be evidenced in:

- the degree of student happiness within the school;

- the positive interaction across the year groups within the school;

- mature and good quality staff-student relationships within the school;

- how the school's students are perceived by the wider public;

- the outcome of surveys conducted among senior students in the school.

### *Endnotes*

Many ideas in this appendix have been informed by Ryan and Bohlin, *Building Character in Schools* Jossey-Bass, San Francisco (1999)

# Appendix 2
# Developing and maintaining a Catholic standard

The Catholic Schools Partnership (CSP) has developed very useful templates for schools at both primary and secondary level to help them review and continually renew what it means to be a Catholic school.

These resources provide a scaffolding to help schools revisit their mission statement (or characteristic spirit) and see how it is being implemented across the school in an ongoing way. The process replicates the approach schools take with regard to other whole school processes, and involves a lot of engagement with all the stakeholders.

As all schools have many levels of involvement with people, with persons having varying degrees of commitment, there is a possibility that consultative processes can become overwhelming. That said, since all Catholic schools already effectively have a defined characteristic spirit, the issue should rather be that of exploring what that spirit means and finding the best ways to promulgate it within the school community. To be really worthwhile, rather than it being a once-off process or event, a review process should happen on rolling basis, perhaps over a five or six-year cycle. Ultimately, a good quality review could happen under the auspices of one or two parents, spread, say, over their children's cycle in the school, backed up by the board of management.

Parents should not be slow in volunteering to contribute to such ethos-supportive initiatives. Deferring to teachers – many of whom may feel too busy to undertake such tasks – may not bring the desired results. The US experience would appear to indicate that professional education bodies have easily succumbed to the prevalent woke culture, making it difficult for any teachers to adapt counter-cultural stances. If such circumstances were to prevail here, it might be easier for parents rather than teachers to take on the responsibility for advancing the school ethos.

Parents who may be reluctant to commit precious family time should consider two things: (a) In this present age, getting value from the school ethos which they have chosen actually requires that parents do provide a strong lead and (b) time invested in the school on this task equates to time invested in educating one's family, and so is not wasted.

The process outlined by the CSP for primary schools includes forty indicators – divided across five key characteristics – as to what makes a Catholic school Catholic. Many primary schools are engaging with this process which is coordinated at a diocesan level. A resource pack with a similar title has been prepared also for secondary schools, which has a somewhat shorter checklist. The five key characteristics around which primary schools are encouraged by the CSP to measure themselves are:

- We are called to be followers of Christ
- We have a Catholic understanding of education
- The school is a Christian community
- The school is an agent of personal growth and social transformation
- Religious education is an integral part of the life of the school.

The recommended CSP approach for secondary schools is to identify targets to facilitate ethos conversations within the school. These targets are gathered together under three key headings:

- Our school's identity and distinctiveness are rooted in its founding story, and the life of the school reflects the inspiration and values of that story
- Our school continues the ministry of Christ
- Our school is in dialogue with the Church and the world around us.

It is envisaged that the targets can be expanded and adapted as schools advance in their reviews.

This book should provide useful supportive ideas and materials which can inform those processes within schools.

Of course, alternative approaches can be taken. For example, if the process is being led by school staff then a school might decide to concentrate on becoming a character education school, and seek to build its Wellbeing programme

## Appendix 2

around character development modules, imbuing additional Christian values as required. Another school might begin by reviewing how it approaches the teaching of morality across all the subject curricula and in this way also help make staff aware of key Catholic principles in that regard. Another school might start by looking at what a holistic education means in the context of their school, paying particular attention to the moral and spiritual formation the school provides. A school might even begin by undertaking a review of specific external programmes provided to the school to see how these programmes align with Catholic principles. A school confident that it is achieving a high standard, might over time look at how it is addressing any or all of the twelve weaknesses identified in Chapter 11.

There are some additional ideas worth reflecting on which can be an encouragement to schools seeking to develop and maintain a Catholic standard within their school. These include:

- The most important first step is for the school to publicly commit to continually refine its ethos. This gradually empowers those who value that commitment to make their contribution to the task.

- It only takes a few school parents with a clear perspective on this task to drive it within any school, building up support as their work progresses. It is much easier to start small, to find one's way and to build up momentum over time.

- When operating in a counter-cultural climate it is very easy to be dragged along by the culture. Mistakes will undoubtedly be made. However, once these are recognised for what they are, schools require a determination to get their characteristic spirit back on track, if they are not to sully the Catholic brand.

- For improvements to be of lasting value the school's trustees and Board of Management need to be committed to working steadily on key school policy documents which can over time filter down into the classroom, into parent meetings and into the staffroom. They also need to provide full backing to any ethos committees set up within the school.

- The school management needs to help its staff to be proud of the school ethos, while being aware of other pressures on some staff to not be fully accepting of it.

- It is important that the ethos be regularly shared with parents without overcomplicating that process. The school should not make claims that it cannot stand over, as this can breed cynicism with regard to the school ethos. It is much better to be on a journey of improvement than to falsely claim success.

- The school management should ask itself whether the characteristic spirit is evident across the whole curriculum, whether there are any discordances, and if so, to consider how these can be corrected. Teachers may need to be supplied with additional supportive curriculum material which may be available from the Catholic Schools Partnership or from Catholic teaching training agencies or other groups. Where such support is not obviously available school management should have a natural expectation that appropriate Catholic or other professional agencies would work to supply these.

- Schools which focus on character education as part of their overall education ethos are not only providing a holistic education but they are helping to create common cause within the whole school community.

- While it is natural for children who share cultures to hang out together within the school environment, schools should be practical and persevering in encouraging students from different backgrounds to mix better with each other. Students need to be helped broaden their friendship groups so that a Catholic openness to others is carried into our wider society.

- Schools may need to seek the expertise of other schools in dealing with more complex matters arising around ethos. Schools required to publicly defend their Catholic ethos should never be made feel that they are alone in the task.

- At all costs, schools need to avoid becoming political spaces if school unity is to be maintained. In particular, at the present time, issues such as race, gender, equality versus equity, and sexual behaviour have all become

# Appendix 2

deeply politicised. Dressed up in social justice garb such movements may be alluring, but may operate in a deeply un-Christian fashion. To that end, organisations which do not respect the overall school mission – even if funded by the state – or which promote intersectional political solutions at the expense of fundamental democratic freedoms – are not groups which should be allowed access to the school.

- Finally, it is worth recalling that many of the mistakes Catholic institutions made in past in Ireland happened when the institutions aligned themselves with the prevailing external culture rather than with Gospel values which could have helped change that culture. Schools which are currently finding it difficult to see beyond the short-term cost of being counter-cultural should cast an eye to the long-term future to realise the real importance of the struggle to present Gospel values. Clear Catholic counter-cultural approaches are what society most needs from its schools at the present time. The 'thank-you for your service' may not be forthcoming for some time to come.

### *Endnotes*

See www.catholicschools.ie for all Catholic Schools Partnership resources. These include two CSP publications *Ethos Process – Understanding and Living the Ethos in a Catholic Primary/Postprimary School.*

# Index
# Our School is Catholic
(abbreviated topics index)

**A**

*A Man for All Seasons*, 172

abuse, 21, 28

academic excellence, 110-112

academic virtue, 111-112

active citizen/citizenship, 148, 163, 171, 177

alcohol abuse, 103, 210

anonymity (student) 92

Aquinas, Thomas, St, 98

Aristotle, 57, 111, 115

Arizona, 180, 181

artificial intelligence, 61

assembly (school), 92, 143

assessment, 106, 113-114, 180-181, 188

atheist, 47, 57

Atheist Ireland, 193-194

Augustine, St, on virtue, 120-121

autonomy, personal, 47, 56, 67, 69, 162, 164, 168, 189, 190, 191

autonomy, school 162

Auschwitz 117

**B**

Benedict, Pope, 72, 77, 78, 80, 97, 101, 107, 128, 130, 163, 168

Biden, 44, 199

Blessed Sacrament, 136

board of management, 141-142, 178, 188, 202, 221-225

book of nature, 158, 179

brand (Catholic), 85, 89-90

bully, 150, 160, 163, 175, 178, 189

**C**

CAO, 17, 110, 131

*Catechism of the Catholic Church*, 129

Catholic education, 18, 23, 24, 57

Catholic education, demand for, 20-21

Catholic failures, 21, 23, 82, 90, 100, 122, 175

Catholic school, definition, 10, 12, 20, 192, 200

Catholic Schools Partnership, 141, 221-225

Census, 17, 20, 30, 31

character education, 10, 98, 105, 115-123, 163-164, 207-219

characteristic spirit/ethos, 13, 20, 29, 53, 77-80, 85, 88-89, 91, 95-97, 126, 141, 143, 147, 186-196, 201, 203, 221-225

charity/love/care, 11, 12, 32, 38-39, 64, 67-68, 73, 75, 100-102, 120-121, 190, 196

chastity, 102, 155, 216

Christian worldview, 46-47

Citizens Assembly (education policy), 171

clash of culture, 28, 86-90, 104-105, 147, 151,152

clericalism, 41, 78

Communism, 50, 103,104

compassion, 68, 100, 104, 151

Comte, Aguste, 35

conscience, 24-25, 39, 47, 48, 74, 104, 121, 189, 192, 204

consent, 158-159

consequentialism, 49

Constitution (Irish), 24, 54, 66, 88, 150, 185

Covid-19, 11, 49, 67, 110

CPD, 142, 144

creed/belief (Catholic), 38-39

critical theory (see woke) 170,172

culture of death, 69-70, 99

curriculum, 11, 99, 102, 105, 121, 124-133, 152, 201, 216

Curvino and Fischer, 156

**D**

democracy needs Christianity, 62-70

democratic roots, 63-65

demographics, 137

Department of Education, 105, 109, 111, 130, 140, 178, 188, 204

DES Inspectorate quality framework, 109, 111

diocesan advisors, 130

diversity, 11, 153, 173, 201

divestment (of schools), 11, 19, 81, 90, 142, 202

Duff, Frank, 21, 102

Dunbar number, 211-212

**E**

Ecology, 35

Edmund Burke, 176

Educate Together 144, 186-194

education, purpose/aim, 8-9, 54, 72, 74

*Education Act, 1998*, 54, 89, 153-154, 161, 189, 200

equality, 50, 58, 64, 73, 187,189

ERB, 55, 149-150, 162, 165-169, 200

ESRI, 157

Ethics, 55, 81, 149-150, 162, 165-169, 200

Ethos (see characteristic spirit)

*EU Convention on Human Rights*, 203

**F**

faith, 19, 31, 32, 38, 79, 82, 87, 98, 131, 200

*Framework for Primary School Curriculum* (draft), 17, 42, 128,

# Index

148-150, 165-169, 170

Francis, Pope, 82, 134, 136-137, 158

free market, 65, 69

free speech, expression, 49-50, 55, 70, 99, 174-176

freedoms, 24, 49-50, 70, 99, 119, 122, 137, 152-153, 175

functionality (of education), 8, 35, 55, 56, 57, 75, 79

## G

GDP (and GNI), 18

gender, identity, ideology, 152, 181, 182, 183, 186, 190, 199

Gladys Ganiel, 32

Good Samaritan, 101

Gospel, 22, 31, 82, 130, 155

grace, 120-121

*Grow in Love*, 129

guidance, 163

## H

history, 29, 38, 64, 176

holistic, 8, 89, 92, 103, 116, 141, 148, 154, 161-162, 188, 200, 223

home-school, 20

Hong Kong, 19

hostility 28-29

## I

*in loco parentis*, 161, 178, 182, 189

inclusion/inclusive, 73, 93, 137-138, 149, 181, 186

Individualism, 190

indoctrination, 175

innovation 105-106

integral, 8, 40

Intersectionality, 170, 174, 176-177

INTO, 183

investment in education, 15, 18

Irish Episcopal Conference, 128-129

## J

Jesus Christ, 22, 24, 37, 39, 63, 73, 78, 97-98, 100, 103, 110, 129, 133-134, 167, 191, 222

John Paul II, Pope St, 99, 135

Junior Cycle, 17, 88, 111, 113, 130, 143, 161-162

justice, 73, 101

## K

Kennedy, Finola, 102

Kennedy, John F, 43

Kilcoyne, Fr Brendan, 12

## L

language (use of), 11, 53, 58, 175, 189

leadership, 75, 88, 91, 102, 106, 122, 142, 210, 217

learning difficulties, 118-119, 181

Leaving Certificate, 17, 19, 89, 92, 105, 107, 110, 113, 130, 131

Legion of Mary, 21, 102

liberal democracy, 63-70

lifelong learning, 138

liturgy / liturgical, 97-98

## M

Martin, Archbishop Eamon, 81-82, 133, 155

Marxism/Marxist, 57, 171-172, 173

Mass (and attendance), 30, 31, 96

meaning and purpose (in education), 50, 72-73

media, 21, 28-29, 33, 87, 90, 198, 199, 204

mental health, 30, 32, 113, 125, 163

morality, 47, 63, 66, 74, 106, 117, 119, 189-190

moral reasoning, 47, 49, 100-101, 103, 162, 189

Mother and Baby Homes, 21, 90

Murray, Dr John, 131

## N

Nationalism, 29

NCCA, 17, 129, 143, 148, 150, 152, 154, 155-157, 165-166, 168, 200, 201

New York, 182

New Zealand, 21

newly qualified teachers (NQT), 144-145

Newman, John Henry (St), 112, 116-117, 121-122, 125-126, 134

Northern Ireland, 19

## O

OECD, 17, 18, 106

Oireachtas, 152

Oregon, 179-180, 181

## P

parents, (incl. parental choice) 16, 17, 32, 54, 81, 124, 200, 208-209, 200, 221-224

parents (primary educator), 23, 24, 25, 89, 91-92, 122, 154, 157, 181-182, 183, 191-192, 194, 212-213, 218

parish, 18, 32, 92-93, 138, 202, 218

patriotism, 29

Patron's Programme, 129, 150, 165, 167

Paul VI, Pope, St, 134

pedagogy, 105, 163, 167, 175, 179-180, 191, 192, 196

personality traits, 117-118, 211

Pew Research Center, 31

piety (see prayer), 97, 133-137, 165

PISA, 18, 22, 106

pluralism, 43-45

Poland, 199

political correctness, 31, 55, 56, 174

prayer (see also piety), 97, 134-137

Programme for Government, 16,

# Index

17, 20, 150, 159, 171

propaganda, 127

pro-life/abortion/unborn, 32, 44, 58, 69, 99, 195-196, 199

public square, 37, 42-45, 48-49, 70, 174

### R

racism, 58, 173, 174, 179

reason, 35, 39, 49, 74, 81, 103, 131, 196

Relationships and Sexuallity Education (RSE), 17, 151-160, 183, 195, 199, 201, 204, 216

relativism, 56, 65

religion, 8, 36, 37, 38, 42-45, 46, 55, 56, 62, 73, 166, 167, 187

religious education (subject) 80, 98, 121, 128-131, 133, 149, 192, 194, 204, 222

reputation, 19

respect, 39, 58, 67, 149, 154, 166-167, 174

### S

sacraments (incl Communion, Reconciliation), 81, 82, 136, 138, 202, 203, 204

safe space (politics in school), 178

Schleicher, Dr Andreas, 106

school and home, 91, 129, 207-219

school as professional environment, 140-145

school, co-education, 187; democratic run, 188; mixed/single sex, 188

schools multi-denominational 20, 186, 189, 202

schools non-denominational/ secular, 193-194, 195, 199, 202, 203

school size (incl. class size), 92, 106, 211-212

science, 26, 44, 49, 51, 55, 80, 112, 127, 162

Scotland, 51

sectarianism, 51

secularism, 28, 35, 42-45, 46, 48, 50-51, 55, 62, 69, 75, 78, 93, 96, 99, 105, 147, 181-182, 194, 196, 198, 203, 205

secularity, healthy, 41, 79

self-evaluation, 109-110

Senior Cycle (see also Leaving Certificate), 130

separation of church and state, 36, 41-43, 65, 147

sexual morality, 99, 100, 179

sex education (see RSE), 195

sexuality, 127, 169, 183

*Share the Good News: National Directory for Catechesis in Ireland*, 129

sin, original sin, 37, 63, 121, 177

social justice, 148, 181

Stephen Bullivant Survey, 31

subjects, number of, 112, 116, 124

subsidiarity, 64

## T

teachers, 109, 113, 120, 122, 128, 175, 183, 191, 193, 202, 204, 208, 215, 217, 221, 224

teachers (as professionals), 140-144; mobility 142, induction, 142

Teaching Council, 140, 143, 181

temperaments, 117-118, 210

Teresa of Calcutta, St, 101

*The Idea of a University*, 125-126

third-level education /colleges/university, 23, 51, 55, 58, 88, 105, 112, 121-122, 125-126, 142, 173, 175, 177, 209

three Rs, 80

throwaway culture, 23, 158

tolerance, 44, 45, , 16673, 81

Treaties (UN / Human rights / Agencies), 47, 48, 49, 51, 64, 148, 153, 155-156, 189, 194-196, 199

truth, 65-66, 73-74, 75, 77- 80, 104, 113, 126, 166-167, 168, 190

## U

unions (teacher), 105, 141, 143, 154, 183

unity of knowledge, 11, 75, 112

Universal Declaration of Human Rights, 51, 64, 155, 194

Utopia,103-104, 176, 177, 211

virtue, 74-75, 98, 111-112, 115-124, 159-160, 163-164, 207-219

vision (Catholic), 88, 89, 125, 177, 192-193

voucher system, 201

## W

Wellbeing, 88, 131, 143, 149, 154, 159, 161-164, 165, 222

WHO, 153, 156-157, 159, 191

William sisters, 119

woke thinking, 11, 30, 49, 50,61, 68, 101, 104, 113, 162, 172-183

worldviews, 10, 53, 54, 57, 61, 63, 64, 99, 104-105, 141, 144

worldviews compare), 46-51

# SOWHAT IMPRINT

SOWHAT Imprint reminds Western society of the existence of God and of why, individually and collectively, we need Him.

## Available now from www.sowhat.ie

**God exists – So What?**
Belief in God is the most natural thing in the world. In this exciting and challenging book the author demonstrates how we can be sure of God's existence.
*'[A] great resource for anyone who wishes to investigate the rationality of theism, whether for personal or professional reasons… I would love to see all my students read this book – both for their own information and inspiration, but also as a source of ideas for teaching.'*

**Escaping the Bunker: Democracy Needs Christianity – So What?**
The survival of democracy itself may depend on Christian commitment. Democracy needs to escape the bunker of pure or unenlightened reason and welcome again the light and heat of Christianity.
*'It logically explores the political landscape and encouragingly points to a way forward to restore the damaged fabric of democracy on the basis of the Christian values on which it is based.'*

**Our School is Catholic – So What?**
Catholic schools have a great pedigree but are under threat from the wider secular culture. This book is a call to schools to commit to being truly Catholic and points the way forward.

For more information or to participate in SoWhat forums or events see **www.sowhat.ie.**

**All the above titles are primarily available through the website shop. To get in touch email admin@sowhat.ie**